HOME
and away

For Mikki

*And to my friends at the SPCA, who will
receive a portion of the royalties from this book.*

*A portion of the royalties will also be donated
to the Saanich Peninsula Hospital's
Palliative Care Facility.*

GLAMORGAN GROUP
watercolour ❧ *Molly Lamb Bobak*

HOME *and away*

more tales of a heritage farm

ANNY SCOONES

VICTORIA · VANCOUVER · CALGARY

ANNABELLE, ANNY AND OLGA, A NAKED NECK CHICKEN
photo by Jacqui Thomas

ANNY SCOONES is a second-term councillor for the District of North Saanich, B.C., with a special interest in heritage and agriculture preservation; parks, trails and cycling paths; and architectural design and planning. She has a B.Ed. in history from the University of Victoria and a Diploma of Humanities in philosophy. At the time of writing, Anny had seven cats and four dogs, all from the SPCA. She continues to ride her Russian woolly horse, raise rare Gloucester Old Spot pigs and collect eggs from her many breeds of hens. Her greatest pleasure is to sit down by the fire in the living room, surrounded by books, candles, flowers, art, bowls of fruit and happy dogs, to think and enjoy being at home.

introduction   vii

i. home

orphans   1

egg surprises   13

happy ducks   17

playing rude   19

three games that pigs enjoy   26

cormack o'connor   29

maintaining an outhouse   41

the ferry dance   44

ii. away

the smell of home   53

gavin's list   58

by the dawn's early light…   66

the contraption   80

the lampshade   85

scenes from a little life   90

the beauty of disasters   99

iii. early journeys & memories

flying alone   106

hey, ma!   111

all you can eat   115

henry   120

on the road with frankenstein   122

stan   135

the comb   144

the photo album   150

ashes   157

iv. home again

two for one   163

coming along   168

arranging a still life   171

the psychic   174

fedRex   178

APPLES AND BOWL
oil ❧ *Harold Mortimer-Lamb*

introduction

Dear Readers,

I have now owned my beloved historic Glamorgan Farm for six years. You may recall from my first book, *Home*, that I decided to buy the old, rundown place quite spontaneously on a damp spring morning as the dogs and I strolled past on our morning walk and saw the red metal roofs in the mist, the crumbling stone wall around the garden and the gnarled old apple trees badly in need of pruning. The 11 structures, many of them original, monumental log barns built back in 1870, were rotting into the ground.

I remember thinking, "I will save you, you dear old farm!" It seemed to have a dignity that invited me up the long, poplar-lined gravel driveway.

Richard John, a Welshman from Glamorganshire, brought his large family to Glamorgan Farm, where he grew oats and raised cattle. He had over 600 acres then, which is a huge part of North Saanich. The farm today is eight and a half acres.

The most colourful owner of Glamorgan Farm was Sam Matson. He owned it in the 1920s. Oh, how I wish I had known Sam! He loved the arts and built Victoria's Royal Theatre, but what he loved the most was his farm and his prize Jersey cows, which won blue ribbons at the

Saanich Fair. Sam's wife stayed in town, but he had friends out here near the farm. Word has it too that he befriended Mrs. Dunsmuir. Well, I wish Sam knew how I am restoring his farm and barns, and how I saved his old quince bush at the gate, and how I love the Saanich Fair too (but rarely win blue ribbons, as you may also recall from a previous story about my pickled-egg entry!). I might even get a couple of Jersey cows, as pets of course, and name one Sam. They say Jerseys give the best cream.

Sam would love the literary fundraisers I hold in the great barn lofts, and the rare, hardy heritage breeds of livestock I raise, such as the Gloucester Old Spot pig, the woolly Russian Bashkir Curly horse and the Naked Neck hens. I'll be taking my woolly horse, Valnah, to the Saanich Fair this year, and I know I'll think of Sam.

Glamorgan Farm is also home to the Healthy Harvest Co-op, a group of challenged adults who grow heirloom produce, fruit and flowers. I wish you could see the lushness and the size of their cabbages! Beside their rich, fertile plots (fertilized with all sorts of manure!) and two greenhouses is Gavin's wonderful, fragrant herb garden and hedgerow of heirloom tea roses. His herb garden is in a wheel pattern, with fruit trees in the centre and plots of lavender, sage, edible flowers and wild greens cramming and spilling over granite rockeries.

The tradition of having my parents, Bruno and Molly Bobak, illustrate my writing continues. Mum and Dad were Canadian war artists, uniformed, and are now living in Fredericton. Dad sketches the New Brunswick countryside, often on some grassy riverbank, and Mum, her eyes failing, paints watercolours of flowers from their garden. Here on Glamorgan Farm, much of their art hangs on the walls of the old farmhouse (originally the farm workers' lodgings), and some of it is shared with you in this book.

I have bequeathed Glamorgan Farm to North Saanich as a heritage park although, as the years go by, I'd like to share its goodness sooner rather than later, and I hope my books assist me in this endeavour. Some of the stories in this book venture farther from home; they are memories of past homes and journeys. Others are stories inspired by this dear, weathered farm, which, in its gentle way, seems to provoke so many reflections on nature and the human spirit.

␺ Anny

"I am only one of many,
and of small account,
if any…"

STEVIE SMITH

LEFT TO RIGHT: RUBY, ALICE MARY AND SAMMY
photo by Mikki Richards; altered by Jacqui Thomas

orphans

I DON'T USE MY COMPUTER often. I am always afraid that it might blow up, or whistle or honk at me, and I won't know why. But once a week I check the Victoria SPCA website to see if there is any old dog I could offer a country retirement to on Glamorgan Farm. Sometimes, after spotting a photograph of a big, sweet, slobbery dog with a bio such as "Harvey needs your help and love—he was found covered in mange and with a broken leg," I'll call and the people at the SPCA will say, "Oh, no, Anny, he's not a farm dog. He hates cats and will kill chickens. He needs obedience training." But if a dog sounds like a possible candidate, I'll drive into town to meet him or her. Very often I'll come home two hours later with some aging mongrel who has been neglected, injured or abandoned.

The CRD, which stands for Capital Regional District, runs our regional animal-control department (also known as "the dog catcher"). I also check the CRD regularly for orphaned dogs in need of a new home. The kennels are on a hill overlooking Elk Lake, a big, clean, local lake surrounded by forest and trails that is home to rowers, fishers, swimmers and, of course, dog walkers. Bulrushes and reeds grow along the shore, concealing duck and swan nests. Wild currant bushes with their delicate magenta flowers, salmonberries and Indian plum crowd the trails, which are frequented by joggers, strollers and, of course, dog walkers.

The pound is itself old and rundown. Pit bulls and Rottweilers seized from marijuana grow-op houses and tough biker gangs snarl saliva through the bars as you walk down a hallway lined with cold kennels that smell of urine. The pound staff do their best. I can't imagine a more difficult job than seizing abused dogs, but I am very grateful to them, and to the SPCA, for providing me with some of the best companions I could ever wish to meet.

i: norton

One of the greatest dogs I adopted from the SPCA was Norton, a huge, white animal with brown patches. John, my husband at the time, named him Norton because we were obsessed with the old Jackie Gleason TV series *The Honeymooners*, and we already had a rather dim-witted chocolate Labrador named Ralph. Ralph and Norton were the two male characters in the series; their wives were Trixie and Alice. John and I would watch the black-and-white reruns every night in bed, with hot-water bottles soothing our liniment-soaked muscles after the hard labour of the day.

I kept 12 horses and gave riding lessons all day; John was a contractor. He built seawalls using smooth, granite boulders that his excavator's big metal teeth lifted and placed together like a jigsaw puzzle along the blustery sandy beaches of Vancouver weekenders' homes. John never cemented his seawalls together. They were works of art—an architecture of boulders. If a forsythia bush, a big old quince or an ancient fruit tree was in the way, John would dig it out and bring it home. Our property on Galiano Island was full of shrubbery saved from developed sites. We had a massive blooming wisteria from the spot where John had built the Galiano ferry terminal, and a prolific plum tree from the site of the ferry terminal on Mayne Island. Mum called John "The Rock Man."

So John and I would lie in our room at night soothing our aches and pains. Dumb old Ralph would be at the foot of the bed, scratching and itching and making the occasional smell. We lived in a shake-and-shingle shack with no foundation. The old cottage sat right on the soil, and when I vacuumed under our bed, the vacuum would get caught in the acacia branches that were growing through the rotten floor. We didn't really have room for another dog, but I would visit the SPCA while I was in town doing errands, and Norton and I bonded instantly. John was won over when Norton treed a raccoon in the walnut tree beside the chicken coop on the night he arrived.

We soon discovered that Norton loved to swim, and we would take him to the beach at Galiano's Montague Harbour. Ralph came along too, but all he could bear to do was paddle. Ralph had come from the Richmond SPCA, and he had always been nervous of three things—

water, nudity and bathrooms. But Norton loved the water. John and I would shuck fresh oysters and cook them over a beach fire while Norton swam for sticks and Ralph sat quietly contemplating the world.

Sometimes at night, after supper, John would get out his accordion. He sat on the couch or in his Uncle Paul's upright wooden chair and played funny old songs. Ralph and Norton liked the music, and they'd lie at his feet resting after a busy day of roaming the property. Our little stray black cat, Dolly, sat and drooled on the burgundy-velvet wingback chair in the corner beside Uncle Paul's old gramophone, the type with the horn and the wind-up arm. Uncle Paul had been known for playing Mozart on the gramophone on his veranda on Sunday nights when he lived on the island; the people across Active Pass, on Mayne Island, heard the music over the water. "Uncle Paul would eat one apple and six walnuts for Sunday dinner," John told me, "and then play Mozart. We were spanked if we spoke!"

One evening as John played his accordion, Norton began to sing along. He didn't howl (as Ralph did, when he heard the local volunteer ambulance taking somebody to the water taxi in an emergency), but rather hummed in tune, breathing at all the right places. After that, whenever John picked up the accordion, Norton would take his place beside Uncle Paul's wooden chair and prepare for the performance. John and Norton's favourite song was "Today I Started Lovin' You Again" ("and I'm right back where I've really always been").

John and I and the dogs were always awakened at dawn by the piercing crow of our big black hen. She would sit on the fence as the

MONTAGUE
oil ❦ Molly Lamb Bobak

sun rose, flap her wings and crow in the day louder than any rooster we ever owned. Then she would proceed back into her coop and lay her egg, often a double-yolker. Norton loved to guard the henhouse from raccoons, and thanks to him we had many eggs.

Ralph was getting old, and he spent most of his later years sleeping in his basket by the fire. One evening at bedtime, he came into our bedroom as usual. When he lifted his leg on the bed to relieve himself, we knew it was time for Ralph to say goodbye to us and to his dear friend Norton. We buried him under an arbutus tree on a cliff overlooking Montague Harbour, where John was removing some boulders for a seawall. Norton carried on singing, swimming and watching the henhouse.

But eventually he too began to slow down. On one occasion, when Mum was visiting from Fredericton, we took Norton for his usual swim. Mum swam too—it was only March, but she wanted to tell Dad, who was back in the freezing east, that she had done it. When she and Norton emerged from the steel-grey water, both of her big toes were cramped at a 90-degree angle. "Don't tell Bruno about my toes," she insisted. I promised I wouldn't.

After their swim, Norton and Mum and I walked through the cedar forest just down the hill from our house. Mum wanted to do some sketches of a little lane John had made. She called it "the bosky bit." Norton enjoyed the woods, and he sniffed around the mossy, musky ground while Mum sketched in her black book and I looked for mushrooms. When it was time to go, we set off up the lane, but poor

Norton took two steps and then cried in anguish—his hips couldn't take him up the hill.

Mum stayed with him while I went and got the truck. I had to lift him in, and when we got home I gave him some warm broth and settled him by the fire. That night, after Norton had hobbled outside to do his nightly business, we heard him bark. When John went out, he found Norton crying in pain under the walnut tree and gazing up into its branches. High, high above was a fat raccoon. That was the last raccoon Norton ever treed, and our crowing hen became a raccoon dinner within weeks; we found her gristly feet in the mud one morning amongst a mass of feathers. Norton had slept soundly through the night as an old dog should, oblivious to it all.

John and I separated later that year and I moved to a small place in North Saanich that I named, in a fit of fury at John, Ever Lasting Farm. I took Norton with me. The farm was five acres, very flat, and just down the road from Glamorgan Farm, an abandoned and derelict property at the time. Norton spent his days sleeping stiffly by the wood stove or lying outdoors while I tried to dig a garden in the tough, dry clay. As time passed, I stopped taking Norton to lovely but cold Sidney Beach and instead walked him gently in the racetrack field across the road. He ate less and less, and he disappeared for long hours at a time.

There was a stand of pampas grass on the lawn that I'd been trying to kill by throwing sink water on it. One afternoon, after pitching on a bucketful, I was dismayed to find Norton asleep in the centre, under the mass of stiff stems and fuzzy growth. He had made a hidden bed, like the ones Saint Bernards make out of snow.

The rains began in late September, and one night we had a storm to end all storms. The wind howled, and the rain beat so hard against our Pan-Abode that water dripped down the kitchen walls. A huge piece of blue metal let go from the barn roof and crashed onto the driveway. In the morning, boughs and branches lay everywhere. Much of the pampas grass had broken off, and the standing plumes looked like a bunch of wet mops. I decided to cut the whole stand down, and I waded into the centre of it with my clippers. After a moment or two, I saw Norton, dead and looking very peaceful, hidden under this horrid bush that I had tried to eradicate, but which as a deathbed looked so inviting—dry and round and padded with soft plumes. Norton's big head was resting against a flat boulder, and his paws were slightly curled.

When John came to visit the next day—we were friends again by then—we wrapped Norton in a blanket, and John took him back to Galiano, to bury him next to Ralph on the ridge. I stopped trying to kill the pampas grass after that, although I couldn't bring myself to actually encourage its growth. When I moved up the road to Glamorgan Farm, I had a garage sale, and a woman gave me 50 cents a plume for the pampas grass. I know Norton would have understood.

ii: fidel

Not long after Norton died, I adopted Grizzly, a mutt from the CRD pound. I didn't feel drawn to him at first—he was so plain, just normal and hairy, with that orphaned look of emptiness. But the CRD man in his navy-blue uniform loved Grizzly. When they'd picked him up, he told me, the dog had had a drug needle embedded in his paw. "He was sad when we found him, almost depressed. He'd be good on a farm," the man said. He's no Norton, I thought guiltily, but I decided to take the risk.

Back at the farm, Grizzly followed me into the kitchen and lay down on a mat. I lit the fire and cooked my supper—a hamburger made from a cow I had raised named Yum Yum. All the other dogs gathered around for a morsel, but Grizzly stayed on his mat, his eyes closed. He might as well have been back in his barred cell.

None of the other dogs paid much attention to Grizzly, and he paid little attention to the farm or to me. He accompanied us on our walks, but without enthusiasm. He was sad, and seemed resigned—a good dog, but sort of blank, lacking in spirit. At least he didn't chase cats or chickens. After I'd had him a week or so, I decided to change his name to Fidel, for Fidel Castro. They struck me as being grizzled in a rather similar way.

Every afternoon at about 5:00, when the weather is good enough, I sit out on my deck to contemplate the day with a drink and a small bowl of chips. Hairy Fidel would always lie at my feet. I have never been an "eye person," and I've never understood the saying about the eyes being windows to the soul. But one warm summer day on the deck, Fidel looked up at me with big brown eyes full of gratitude and contentment. From that moment onward, he followed me everywhere with a loving loyalty. On one shopping trip to Sidney, he rode in the front seat of the car and, with great dignity, accepted a cookie from the gas-station clerk through the car window.

At the end of that summer, Fidel got a nosebleed that didn't go away. The veterinarian in Sidney diagnosed it as nasal cancer, and Fidel was placed on large white pills. The vets at the clinic are wonderful. One does only birds, including chickens. I once rushed over there with a white hen who had been attacked by a hawk and had her eye pecked out. The hen didn't make it, but the vet was so kind.

That autumn Fidel discovered his love of the seashore. Every day at 5:00, instead of sitting on the deck, we would go to Sidney Beach. He would tear up and down over the smooth pebbles and in among the driftwood, dipping his head in the waves that rolled onto the shore. He'd occasionally come up for air, seaweed draped over his brow, and I would wipe the blood from his nose. The vet couldn't believe that Fidel continued to live such a productive life—I thank the sea.

By late fall, however, as the grey skies hung low, Fidel had stopped eating. He told me one evening, in his eye-contact way, that he was ready to die, and the vet came out the next morning to give him an injection. Fidel died with his head in my lap. Knowing that he was about to go, I'd asked my neighbour, Fred, to come over a few days earlier with his backhoe. The vet helped me lift Fidel into the hole Fred had dug beside a struggling pussy willow. Just before we buried Fidel, I remembered I had two hens to bury too; they had died in the night without warning (hens tend to do that). So I put them in with Fidel. I knew he wouldn't mind, the gentle soul who never asked for anything.

I had a drink in honour of Fidel by the fire that evening. I was so glad I'd been able to give that lonely dog six months of happiness, purpose and love. My friend Jane came up the next day and placed two papier mâché bluebirds on the granite stone marking his grave, because Fidel had loved gazing at the birds as he lay under a shady maple in the summer heat. The two bluebirds disintegrated in the winter rains, as I am sure Fidel did also, buried deep in the clay.

iii: old gals—must stay together

Soon after Fidel's death I visited the Victoria SPCA's web page. Down at the bottom, under all the pictures of pit bulls and shepherd/Rottweiler, Lab and collie crosses, was a photograph of two fuzzy smiling mongrels in a basket. The caption read, "Two Old Gals—Must Stay Together." Then: "We are from Quesnel, where we were given up. We are sisters and bonded and quite old, still looking for our forever home."

I had room for the two old girls on Glamorgan Farm.

The only female dog I had was Baby Alice Mary, and I took her with me to the SPCA in the back seat of our van, which is 10 years old and smells terribly of wet dog from years of beach walks. Baby Alice stayed in the van while I went inside.

"I should warn you," the nice SPCA lady said, "that the gals are smaller than they look in their picture, and they are old." She unlocked kennel number 14, and there, sitting in a basket, were two tiny mutts with bright dark eyes. Lily and Daisy were lap dogs—each smaller than a chicken—and they were 15 years old. I carried them out to the van, one under each arm.

The Old Gals are still on Glamorgan Farm, and they sleep under my desk when I work. Daisy learned to swim, at Pat Bay, when she was 16. In the summertime, when live harness racing takes place across the road at the Sandown racetrack, and all the grooms pull their mobile homes in for the season, Daisy and Lily often go over and sit at the steps of one of these vehicles, looking longingly at the flimsy aluminum door. My theory is that they lived in a trailer park in Quesnel, with a little old lady in a pink polyester dressing gown. After the lady died, her son, who lived in a city somewhere and wasn't partial to dogs, gave Daisy and Lily to the SPCA.

Daisy and Lily greet visitors to Glamorgan Farm with bright eyes and wagging tails, and they love to make the farm rounds with me every morning. We fill the duck pools with fresh water, give the hens their corn, groom the horses, put the eggs out for sale, collect the morning paper and talk to the goats.

Last Christmas, Daisy had a minor stroke in the van as we were going to the beach. Lily developed polyps in her throat. But with quiet nursing and gentle walks on the shady trail at the corner of Glamorgan Road, both old girls recovered. They like nothing better than to lie in the tall grass beside the woodpile, watching the world go by—together, just as the SPCA said they should be.

egg surprises

COLLECTING AND SELLING EGGS IS one of the most relaxing and rewarding activities on Glamorgan Farm. There is a surprise every time you do it. What will you find? A blue egg? A double-yolker? Chickens don't lay every day—that would exhaust them—and they take the winter off to rest. But come spring they start up again. To encourage them, I give them fresh hay every morning in their private nesting boxes.

The delicate Polish Crested hens, who lay white eggs, sport plumes that look like the hats the Queen Mother used to wear to the horse races at Ascot. The Naked Neck hens, a very rare breed that originated in Hungary when a farmer bred a hen to a turkey, have long, red, wrinkled necks and lay large brown eggs. My oldest Naked Neck, Olga, is 13. The Araucana are large, multicoloured hens from South America. Their eggs have blue or green shells. And then there's my dear little red bantam, Jennifer, who hasn't laid an egg in years.

She prefers to spend her days sitting on the barn windowsill. Big Rusty, the Rhode Island Red rooster, is also from a breed now on the rare list. Big Rusty struts around the pen guarding his varied flock and is always the last one to go inside at night, carefully making sure that none of the hens are still outdoors, vulnerable to a raccoon attack.

As chickens are about to lay, they cluck a little and then start squawking, as if to tell the entire planet what they have done. When the egg first appears, it is covered in a thin, clear coating. A hen likes to sit on her egg for a while, and then she leaves. Occasionally, another hen will come along and eat the eggs—I'm not sure why—so I make sure to pick them up regularly.

Chickens have a very full day. Besides laying their eggs and contemplating life for long hours in their hay boxes, they like to have dust baths. First they scratch out a hole, picking at grubs as they go along. Then they roll in the cool soil, and sometimes lie down sideways there and go to sleep. They look positively dead with their scaly yellow legs sticking straight out of the hole.

Here's a good daily egg routine:
1.   Check for eggs regularly throughout the day, beginning at 9:00 in the morning, because different hens have different routines. The last egg is usually laid at about 4:00 PM. Look for eggs not only in the chickens' nesting boxes but under bushes and in secret places. Some hens are very private and don't like to lay in public. Sometimes a hen gets caught short, too, and lays an egg outside.

2.   Don't leave eggs where greedy portly Labradors or other farm dogs can get at them. You might want to crack a fresh egg every so often for the barn cat, though. My cat Annabelle loves them.

3.   Wash your eggs in cool water. Look over each one carefully. An egg may be cracked if the chicken stood up as it landed and the egg hit the surface too hard. Set aside only the clean, well-shaped eggs to sell. Some eggs are very misshapen but still good to eat, so you can save those for yourself.

4.   Dry the eggs and put them in a carton. Arrange the eggs nicely, perhaps in a colour-coded pattern. I like to mix the blue, white, brown and pinkish eggs in a nice design, decorating them with a clean feather and including a sheet that describes the eggs from each breed of hen.

5.   Tie the carton shut with a piece of yarn. If you are selling your eggs outdoors, put them in the shade in a cooler. Make an attractive sign for the road. Mine reads: "Fresh Glamorgan Farm Free Range Eggs from Heritage Hens: $3.00."

6.   Leave a jar for money in the cooler. I have never lost a dozen eggs—people are honest—but one time somebody left two dollars worth of pennies.

7.   Keep your chicken pen raked and tidy so that people can admire your flock when they come to pick up their eggs.

I also have three female ducks on Glamorgan Farm—Jemima, Jewel and Jessica. They lay lovely thick-yolked eggs daily in an out-door nest, and I collect them to make delicious omelettes. Duck eggs are twice the size of chicken eggs, and they contain 25 percent more nutrition. For baking, nothing can compare with them.

When I sell Glamorgan eggs by the dozen, I always include one duck egg with the following explanation: "In my experience, duck eggs make very moist cakes. Cakes made with duck eggs maintain their freshness longer, too, and duck-egg omelettes are lighter and fluffier. Duck eggshells are also less porous than chicken eggs and therefore store better." Despite all of this, most regular customers tell me, "No duck eggs, please." I have never figured out why.

NAKED NECK WITH EGG
watercolour ❧ *Molly Lamb Bobak*

happy ducks

DUCKS HAVE A LOT OF personality. They have a sense of humour and a need for privacy. They grieve and they like affection. They have respect for each other, too. Because ducks show so much emotion, there are many ways to keep them happy. Here are some things that Jewel, Jemima, Jessica and Jake the Drake, the ducks on Glamorgan Farm, enjoy.

1.   Ducks love a clean duckhouse with lots of fresh hay and straw to nest in at night. When my ducks see me cleaning out their house, they gather around with keen enthusiasm, and they spend some time, once I'm finished, arranging the bedding as they like it. A duckhouse should be small, and no light bulb is necessary. Ducks like things dim and cool.

2.   Ducks love a private, even darker, area for their nests, which they create from their down. A duck will sit quietly for days and days in her nest, coming out only for a bath and a meagre meal. And she will leave only if she feels sure that her nest will be safe while she's out. For nesting purposes, I've put an old dog crate in the corner of the duckhouse and covered it with hay.

3. Ducks spend much of their time sitting on a high shelf or platform outdoors, taking in the sun and occasionally catching a passing bug. To really brighten their day, get a garden fork and dig over some mounds of soil: the ducks will have a field day eating the worms and finding other grubs and roots. They'll be standing beside you as you dig, so be careful not to drive your fork through a webbed foot!

4. Another duck treat is wet white bread. I crumble the bread into a pan of fresh water. If you add some worms, your ducks will be in heaven. Gavin, the herb gardener on Glamorgan Farm, gives the ducks bucketfuls of greens and weeds, which they also relish.

5. Of course, a fresh pool of water every day makes a duck very happy. Ducks love to bathe, especially the females, and the deeper the pool the better. A running hose stimulates the bathing process.

6. Ducks waddle indoors on their own at dusk. Let them go in when they are ready—they don't like to be rushed. The ladies go in first and nestle into their beds for sleep. The male stays up and awake until dark, standing at the duckhouse door to protect his flock from nocturnal danger. To allow the male to maintain his self-esteem and confidence, it is important to encourage him in this role.

7. Lastly, ducks enjoy human affection. Jessica, a pretty black-and-white Muscovy who lays an egg almost every day but has no interest in hatching it (she'd rather be an auntie to Jemima's babies), loves to sit on my knee and have her neck gently stroked with my finger. She closes her eyes in pleasure, and I tell her she's a wonderful, beautiful duck. Like people, ducks can't hear this too often.

playing rude

LAST YEAR I BOUGHT A small, red-haired boar I named Boris. He is a Duroc-cross who arrived on Glamorgan Farm in a flimsy, filthy, slatted wire crate in the back of a rusty pickup truck. Boris's wet pink snout was jammed through the slats, and he seemed very nervous.

I was hoping that Boris would eventually mate with Mabel and Matilda, the two rare Gloucester Old Spot sows I had imported. They needed to be bred before they went barren. I had been waiting to hear if I could import Gloucester Old Spot sperm from Patrick, a boar owned by a man in a town called Temple Newsam, England, but the man never answered my inquiries. Crossbreeding would just have to do, I decided, although Boris would need to grow a bit before he could do his duty— he weighed 40 pounds and his two wives-in-waiting each weighed 700!

I worried that Mabel and Matilda would bully their new friend, but when they lumbered in from the meadow where they had been basking in a mud pit amongst the blackberries, they sniffed their guest and thought nothing more of it. They looked up at me with their tiny eyes and V-shaped mouths as if to say, "Well, where's our apple, then?"

Boris had to have a warm iodine bath because he was covered in bugs. I prided myself on the fact that the two big pink girls were sweet-smelling and clean. They did their business far from their eating and sleeping area, and I picked it up every morning with a pitchfork and took it to the compost pile that Gavin, the herb gardener, maintains.

I sponged the squealing red piglet off and then dusted him with lice powder. He went into a pen alone with some pig kibble and a banana, and his future wives had their usual mash and cooked root vegetables, grunting in appreciation with every mouthful.

When dusk fell over the farm, I let Boris out into the meadow with Mabel and Matilda. Everything seemed calm as the three of them ambled through the cool evening grass. I went about my other chores and at sundown returned to check on the new family in the pig barn. Matilda and Mabel were sound asleep in their hay beds, their floppy ears drooping over their eyes and their stout legs jutting out from beneath their great jowls. In between them, I saw a strip of red hair and a pink snout. Baby Boris was sleeping peacefully between the two warm bodies.

I felt a huge love for Matilda and Mabel for accepting this young male into their domain. But pigs are like that. They try to be friends with everyone they meet—the dogs who sniff them through the fencing, the horses who arch their muscular necks over the gates and Annabelle, the calico barn cat who saunters up to the pig barn every morning.

MOLLY WITH EMMA
oil ❦ *Harold Mortimer-Lamb*

My friend Nancy wants to write a book called *Live Like a Pig—Your Guide to Happiness and Contentment.* One chapter would be about being open and friendly and trusting everyone; another would be about how our fear of germs and our overuse of germ-killing soaps and sprays are ruining our immune systems—dirt is good and nothing to be afraid of. There would be a chapter saying that it's okay to be overweight, and one extolling the benefits and pleasures to be gained from sleep.

Boris soon became a real favourite around the farm. He loved to have his belly rubbed, and he *ran* everywhere, never walked. As he ran, he squealed with joy. Months passed, and Boris grew into a large, robust chap with shiny copper hair and round, muscular hips (hams).

But company was all that Boris seemed to desire from Mabel and Matilda. He played with his ball, stood still to be brushed, ate bananas, nibbled on blackberries, made friends through the fence with Scruffy, the donkey next door, lay in his mud baths and had his little thinks—he did everything but his manly duty. The two Old Spot sows gazed at him with affection, but Boris would run off in the other direction to look at a butterfly. Here was another chapter for the *Live Like a Pig* book, Nancy and I thought. Some creatures like to dream and contemplate nature, and have very little desire to procreate.

Mum came out to the farm from Fredericton for a two-week visit that summer. One night we got a little giddy on the deck, and I said to her, "I don't what I'm going to do about Boris. He just isn't interested in breeding."

Mum said, "Bless his little heart," which was no help at all.

Mum had told me once that when she was small and living on Raeside Drive in Vancouver, she, her best friend Barbara from next door and a little neighbour named Cedric used to go into the forest and "play rude."

"Play *what?*" I asked.

"Play rude," said Mum, as she sipped her Scotch. "We did it with dandelions on our bottoms," she explained, in gales of laughter, "and we called it Tinkle Berry Wood. Cedric would go home and tell and then we were all confined to our gardens for days, until our mothers forgot. And then we would go into the wood and play rude again."

To my surprise, one morning during Mum's visit, I spotted Boris playing rude with Mabel in the corner of the field. As soon as he saw me with a banana, though, he abandoned her and came running and squealing for his treat.

The cold, rainy winter passed. I gave the piggies extra kibble and more hay to build up their beds, which they spent hours doing with their thick, strong snouts. There were days when it was so grey and raw that they did their business right beside their door, which created a foul-smelling quagmire. I spent hours shovelling the mud and putrid slush away from their entrance and digging drainage ditches. Finally spring arrived, bringing lighter days and sprigs of new green growth. Mabel, Boris and Matilda ventured once again into the meadow.

One morning I awoke earlier than usual, since I planned to go to Galiano Island for the day. I went about my chores briskly, then loaded the dogs into the van. I'd decided to feed the piggies last, and after I'd mixed some cooked potato and chard in their buckets, I lugged them up to the barn. Boris and Matilda were outdoors already, sniffing the damp air. Mabel ambled out when she heard me calling, "Good morning, piggies!" (Nobody ever really says, "Suuuuuu—eee!") All three followed me into the concrete section, where I dumped the buckets and they dove in.

I filled the pigs' black rubber water bucket, then cut open a fresh bale of straw, tossing an armload into their bedding area for them to fluff up later. As I did, I heard a pathetic little squeal. There, in the straw bed, were four tiny, shivering, pink-spotted creatures. I looked in amazement at Mabel, who was heartily gobbling down her potato, and noticed that she had developed huge, soft, pink milk bags. I looked over at Boris, who I swear winked at me.

And then panic set in. Heat lamp! Umbilical cords to be dipped in iodine! Some expert somewhere to be informed that the first

PIG
pen and ink ❧ *Bruno Brobak*

Gloucester Old Spot offspring had been born in Canada! I'll miss the ferry, I thought. And there were Mabel and Boris, calmly eating their potatoes. Matilda, who I now saw was looking a little plump herself, chewed happily, a piece of chard dangling from her bottom lip.

Mabel soon lay down to nurse in the bed of new straw. I set up the heat lamp, and the four little piglets cozied down onto a choice of 14 succulent nipples. Mabel drifted off into a deep sleep, and I went off to Galiano.

I named the four boy piglets Boris Junior, Alexander, Nicolai and Gorby. Gorby had a large spot on his forehead. Boris Junior was soon a holy terror, getting into everything. He pulled the heat lamp down, bit his brothers' ears and tormented his tired mother by wanting to try every teat for a better slurp.

Two weeks later, Matilda gave birth to 10 piglets. It was difficult for her. Her bed was a mess of blood and fluid, and the pale, weak runt died. I buried its tiny corpse in my rockery of heritage roses.

With all these new piglets to raise, I gave Boris away to a nice family who needed him to service their pig, Penelope. He went off in a trailer to Langford to continue his crucial job of playing rude, which he obviously preferred to do in absolute privacy.

three games that pigs enjoy

MY GLOUCESTER OLD SPOT PIG Matilda has an affectionate nature and quite a sense of humour. Her sister, Mabel, is a bit more reserved.

When Matilda was a small pig, she and I used to play a form of tag. I would attempt to grab her flopping pink ears as she tossed her head from side to side, trying to avoid me. When she had had enough, she would indicate that the game was over by raising her head and opening her V-shaped mouth to expose a couple of white teeth, her way of asking for a banana or a piece of cooked yam.

Matilda and I can't play tag anymore because she has grown to weigh 700 pounds and can knock me over with one swipe of her snout. But here are three games that still amuse us both:

1. The Chair Game

This is a simple game for one pig and one person. The person sits on the lawn in a plastic lawn chair while the pig rubs her body against the chair. The person interprets this as the pig trying to get her out of the chair. The pig interprets the game as a way of both scratching and getting attention. The person usually ends up on the ground, and the pig may toss the chair around for a few minutes. The game is over when the person scratches the pig behind the ears and says, "Fine, pig—you win."

2. The Wheelbarrow Game

This game, which Matilda and I discovered inadvertently, is a real thrill for pigs. The fuller the wheelbarrow, the better.

Wheel your barrow into the pigpen and fork in rocks and pig manure for a while as the pig watches. Then stand beside the barrow and lay down your fork so the pig will know you are finished. Very soon the pig will approach and take great delight in tipping over the barrow with her snout.

The game is not yet over, however. The pig will proceed to rub against, push and flip the wheelbarrow until the metal handles are bent, the wheel is flattened and the whole thing falls apart. It's more fun for the pig if you try to rescue the barrow before it is destroyed. The pig finds this highly comical and will push the barrow every way she can to prevent you from wheeling it out of the paddock.

You win if you can leave, only mildly frustrated, with your

barrow intact and the pig still inside the fence. You get bonus points if you leave with any of the barrow contents.

3 . The Shower Game

Pigs like to keep their skin cool, and they love to be hosed down on a hot day. Get a hose attachment that has a shower setting. Stand in the field with the hose on and call, " P. . I. .I. .I. .G … !"

The pigs will waddle out and squirm with pleasure under the spray. But the game is not over until you fill a bucket or two and set it on the ground for the pigs to tip over in a cavalier manner. That way, they will get not only a cool shower but a muddy spot to snout around in as well. The winner of the game is the one who walks away the least exasperated and either the driest or the wettest, depending on your perspective.

No matter what happens, you'll be left there alone in the field, covered in mud, with a bunch of buckets to clean and a hose to roll up and put away. That may make you feel you have lost the game, until you realize you're always a winner—just by being lucky enough to have pigs.

cormack o'connor

FOR SEVERAL YEARS, I RAN a small riding school on Glamorgan Farm. I had a few old horses—some people would call them "nags"—with sunken flanks and long teeth. They were dependable, placid, hardy and patient—"bomb proof," in horse terms—and they would droop their great tired heads as the students, mainly young girls, combed their faces and forelocks, wiped a warm sponge around their eyes, or brushed their coarse tails with a peppermint detangling lotion.

Even though they are never the prettiest or most well-bred horses in the neighbourhood, these "school horses" are to be honoured for their kindness, gentleness and wisdom. The little girls adored them. They rode the horses after school, around the farm's sandy riding ring with its white-railed fence or on a well-worn trail across the road behind the Sandown racetrack.

I am a great believer in discipline, both with the riding itself and with the care of the horses. If it had been raining, each rider was required upon her return to towel off her horse, dry its heels to prevent chapping, and paint its hooves with a special cream to prevent dryness and hoof rot, or thrush. Blankets were strapped onto the thinner horses to keep them from getting chilled. After all of the horses were safely in their stalls with their hay, water and grain, each rider was to clean the grooming tools she'd used, then oil her saddle and wash off the bit, the metal part of the bridle that goes in the horse's mouth.

Each horse had its own saddle rack, bridle hook and grooming tray, and each area was neatly labelled in blue enamel paint: Monty, Anastasia, Japonica, Minny, Napoleon, Kyle, Yuri, Duke, Valnah, Hasu, Sofie and Cormack O'Connor. Parents would arrive at the farm on their way home from work, dressed in business suits, to pick up their children. When the last student had departed, I'd shut off the barn lights to the sounds of the horses munching their hay and passing gas. They were contented after making so many little girls happy.

Every morning, the horses would be stomping in their stalls, hungry and anxious to get out into the field where they rolled to cool their skin, caking themselves in mud and North Saanich clay. I'd throw a large flake of hay into each stall, along with a bucket of grain, then fill the water buckets with the hose. While the horses ate, the dogs and I fed the chickens and ducks, checked the property for wind damage and then went inside to eat our own breakfast.

Throughout the day I cleaned the stalls and figured out what we would do in the riding lessons after school. Sometimes I drilled the students hard with figure-eights and difficult bareback exercises to improve their balance, but on other days we just had fun, playing games on horseback or riding over to the racetrack. I always organized an Easter egg hunt, hiding foil-wrapped candy eggs earlier in the day in the trees and shrubs, or in the barn gutters, or under stones. One year the crows beat the riders to them.

Some of the fondest memories of my riding-school years involve the Saanich Fair. We would always attend, taking pains with our preparations. One year we decided to make a mural for each horse, which we planned to nail to the stalls, embellishing them further with swaths of cloth and bouquets of plastic flowers.

The murals were painted on plywood, and some had additional items affixed with a hot-glue gun. It was great fun. A girl who loved the Russian woolly horse, Valnah, painted his head on the mural and then glued on grey lint from the dryer to represent his wool. Another rider painted Minny, an elegant black mare who loved to stride along the beach at Pat Bay; the girl glued sand dollars, seashells and driftwood onto the mural in among Minny's galloping legs. Another girl depicted Yuri, a big strong Palomino, jumping a stone wall in the woods; pine cones, branches and small pebbles created a west coast forest effect. And Cormack O'Connor, a huge white horse with kind eyes and a pink nose, was portrayed at night, sleeping in a meadow, under a large, round, tinfoil moon.

Cormack O'Connor was old and haggard and patient, perfect for nervous children or beginner ladies, of which I had four. The lady riders called themselves the "Buckerettes" and, truth be known, they spent more time during their lessons drinking martinis, gossiping and reading fashion magazines beside the hot tub than doing any actual riding. But they enjoyed themselves greatly, and they would moan about their aches and pains as they slid off the horses and drove home to their families in town.

My friend Jane, the original Buckerette, had found Cormack O'Connor through an ad in a local horse magazine. Kaspar, as he was called then, had come from an auction and was living at a barn in Maple Ridge, a small city east of Vancouver. Jane and I took the ferry to the mainland to meet him. It was a rainy day, and we drove through endless suburbs filled with pink stucco houses and dwarf cedar hedges, through some industrial sections, and then into a pleasant pastoral area after taking another little ferry across the muddy Fraser River.

The stable where we were to see Kaspar was enormous. A line of horse trailers stood in the gravel parking lot, and a few wet horses were grazing in a soggy meadow bordered by an alder wood. Inside the unpainted barn were row upon row of horses, each in a stall lit with a bare light bulb. Kaspar was easy to spot—his white face and pink nose were larger than any other horse's.

It was love at first sight between Jane and Kaspar. Jane wrote the cheque for him within 10 minutes to a man in jeans and a cowboy hat. On our way home, she announced, "I will rename him Cormack O'Connor, after the famous Irish chieftain." (Jane is as obsessed with the Irish as I am with the Russians.)

Cormack O'Connor arrived at Glamorgan Farm a week later. He was far too big for his trailer; his head was bent down, and his rear end was so jammed up against the trailer doors that his tail hung outside. He moved stiffly as he backed off the trailer ramp, and I left him out for the afternoon in a meadow, where he wandered slowly, nibbling the new grass shoots of spring.

Cormack quickly became the favourite horse at the farm. He was a dear, taking nervous students down our North Saanich country lanes, along the Pat Bay beach, where he waded into the water until it lapped to his bony white hips, or for a gentle jog up to the airport meadow, where the tall grass, clover and buttercups reached his spindly knees. The roar of the landing jets, the tour buses along West Saanich Road and the bright-red Coast Guard vessels coming and going in the bay: none of these fazed Cormack O'Connor. At the end of the day, I always gave him an extra apple, which he took with humility, his kind eyes closed from a day of making so many people happy.

The Saanich Fair is always held in late August, and the day before it opened my old pal Fred Ball, known by every horse person in the area, would come to Glamorgan Farm with his eight-horse trailer. The students and their parents and I would have already worked all day at the grounds, decorating the stalls, and then come home to shampoo the horses, oil the saddles and our boots, pack the trays of brushes and coat sprays, and braid the horses' tails and manes with elastics and coloured wool. All of the horses were prepared for the short journey in Fred's trailer by having their legs bandaged with thick woollen wraps, in case one of them lost its balance en route.

As we drove along the little gravel side roads, the horses thumped in the back of the trailer. The horse trailers at the fair are parked in an area near the outdoor arena, which is ringed by dark-green bleachers. As we arrived the year we'd done the murals, the ground of the arena was receiving a fresh layer of cedar chips, which were then watered by a truck with a spraying contraption, to keep the dust down. Next to the horse arena was the llama pen, where a woman in tight jeans was walking four llamas.

In the sheep barn behind the riding arena, the 4-H youth had their sheep tied up to racks. Some of the sheep wore immaculate red coats and were calmly chewing hay in their narrow, busy mouths. Their owners, looking far more dishevelled, combed the thick, white wool with brisk strokes. Cows were being hosed down next to the sheep, their pink udders gleaming.

Women carrying colourful bouquets of dahlias hurried into a new metal building. An array of gigantic pumpkins sat on the back of a wagon, waiting to be weighed for the grand prize. Old men in overalls were firing up their ancient tractors and steam engines over by the ice-cream booth. When one engine blew its whistle, a puff of smoke shot out of a horn.

My excited students, well versed in our procedures by now, put the horses into their assigned stalls, removed and folded up the leg bandages and fed each horse some hay and grain. A group of parents fired up their barbecues, getting ready to feed us. Once the horses were taken care of, my riders unpacked their tents. We were all going to live at the Saanich Fair for the next three days, to take in the spinning rides, compete in riding events, eat nothing but cotton candy, popcorn and candy apples, look after our horses, learn about defeat and victory, cheer each other on, have sponge baths and use the overflowing turquoise porta-potties.

This was the culmination of a year of devotion and work, and we were almost drunk with anticipation. I had made only two rules: no going on rides or eating hot dogs while wearing our white blouses and jodhpurs, and care for the horses had to be completed before going to the fairgrounds. Some of the girls' parents had brought mobile campers, and they set up nearby.

Before bed, full of barbecued hamburgers, the riders and I trudged up to the barns in our pajamas and rubber boots to check on our horses. Then we collapsed into our sleeping bags, ready to be up at dawn to dress, to groom, to compete, to ride the scrambler or the octopus, and to anxiously await the judge's decision on whether or not we would win the stall-decoration rosette.

The next morning I awoke to see a slit of bright sky over the distant hills. The dew on the grass was heavy. There was a crisp, fall smell in the air, and the scent of saturated cedar chips and meadow. The Lions Club caravan down the lane was just starting to brew coffee, and a few muffled cock-a-doodle-doos came from the poultry barn.

When I got to the horse barn, I discovered that Cormack had lain down in the night and now had a manure stain on one hip; we would have to shampoo it off before his first class, "Beginner Walk/Trot." Glassy-eyed riders began to appear from behind the dripping tent flaps. Soon they would be washed and dressed and warming up in the holding area, cardboard numbers pinned to the backs of their navy-blue blazers. But for now, still in their pajamas, they staggered from horse to horse, feeding each one the grain we'd set out in blue buckets the night before and filling the water troughs.

By noon, the sun was beating down on the bleachers and the dusty riding arena. The place was packed with spectators, and in the distance you could hear the shrieks and screams of people being flung upside down and sideways on the rides. The scent of cotton candy filled the air. Best of all, we now had an array of colour-ful rosettes pinned to our stall doors. Cormack hadn't received any, though. The judge, a tall, blonde woman in a turquoise pantsuit trimmed with rhinestones, wearing a fuchsia felt Stetson, didn't like Cormack's "movement," she said, although she told each of his riders, "He is very well behaved."

Just before the lunch break, the judge walked around the barns looking at the stall decorations. We had raked our area clean, set out nice green hay bales, made sure our murals were visible and filled the water buckets. Each of the riders stood beside a stall in her white blouse and polished boots. Their parents gathered in a group at the end of the aisle.

The judge took lots of notes, asked the students questions about our riding club and stroked Cormack's white head. Then she moved on to a fancy barn around the other side, which was adorned with a commercial sign reading "Arabian Dancers—Academy of Riding" in gold letters on a black background. The club had a video playing on the history of the Arabian horse, and members were handing out candy. Each horse's stall was covered in a purple velvet drape with the horse's name embroidered in gold thread and tassels.

The horse show resumed after lunch, and the heat settled in; it must have been over 90 degrees. Cormack had to withdraw from his classes; he was just too tired in the sun, and the dust irritated his weak lungs. He dozed in his stall instead, and we took turns sponging him down.

Around 3:00 a voice came over the loudspeaker. "And now for the winner in the stall-decoration category," it announced. "Please come to the entry booth to pick up your rosette and cash prize." The girls and I sat on the bleachers, waiting with bated breath. The announcer continued, "The winner is . . . the Maple Stryup Riding Club." We leapt and cheered and the students ran up to collect the prize. It was $50 and a pink and purple ribbon that read in gold letters, "Best Stall Decoration—Saanich Fair." We decided to blow the entire amount of our winnings on junk food and rides that evening.

Autumn arrived, with the rains, and the riders continued to come to the farm every day after school. The horses grew thick, furry coats, and we brought their winter blankets down from the loft. In the tack room I turned the heaters on during the day. Cormack carried on in the damp and the fog, plodding patiently over the wet sand and through the puddles. The Garry oaks stood black against the night sky by the time the daily lessons had ended, and Cormack would retire to his stall, where we covered him with a burlap rug and filled his feed bin with steaming bran mash. The riders warmed up with hot chocolate.

Saturdays were always happy times, since the riders were allowed to come out to the farm for the whole day. They'd groom the horses, clean the stalls, oil saddles, sweep out the tack room and, near Christmas, hang wreaths and strings of lights around the stalls and barn.

One Saturday morning in December dawned as the bleakest day of the year so far. Freezing rain beat against the barn. Garry oak limbs had snapped in the night, and they were scattered across the laneways and pastures. The sky was low, a very dark grey. I walked down the barn hallway feeding each horse hay and grain. They nickered in anticipation. The riders had hung fuzzy green and red stockings on each stall door, and these bulged with combs, apples and homemade grain treats.

I didn't see Cormack's white head and pink muzzle, so I looked into his stall. His huge, bony body was sprawled across the straw, his long legs straight out in front. He struggled as I watched but couldn't get up. I'd heard of horses becoming "cast"—not having enough room to rise from lying down—but Cormack seemed to be in physical pain. His eyes were half-closed, and little moaning sounds came from his soft muzzle. I crouched down beside his head and stroked him, and he calmed a little. I could hear the cold rain pounding on the roof.

As the riders began to arrive, Cormack made several valiant, thrashing attempts to get up, but his massive body remained heavily on the wooden floor. I decided to call the vet for help. She was out of town, and her stand-in vet was away on a call. I left a message.

By lunchtime, Cormack had a collection of little girls kneeling around him, stroking his resigned face. "He may die today," I told them. It was obvious that Cormack's hips were injured, maybe broken. I called the vet every hour but kept getting the answering machine. The barn was unheated, and the riders were very cold by 4:00, but they devotedly sat with their beloved Cormack. By then, he was resting his head on the thighs of a little girl named Heather, who had silent tears streaming down her face. I'd finally heard from the vet, and he was on his way. I had decided to put Cormack "to sleep," I told the riders. That was the kindest thing to do. As the parents arrived, they congregated in the tack room, huddled in their coats, while the riders and I kept watch with Cormack.

Finally Heather broke her silence by saying, "Let's open his stocking." Her lips were dark purple by this time, and her thighs under her blue jeans were trembling. The damp, raw chill of night was setting in. We pulled Cormack's stocking off his door, and each rider reached into the green fuzz to pull something out. First came a Granny Smith apple. I sliced it up and everyone gave Cormack a piece. He seemed to enjoy it, raising his lips slightly to each hand. The next present in the stocking was some combs, which the little riders used to comb Cormack's stringy white forelock. One mother anxiously carried in a tray with mugs full of hot chocolate. The tired, sad riders continued to kneel beside their friend as they took off their gloves and drank. They got cocoa all over their faces.

The vet arrived, a tall, serious man carrying a black leather bag. I told the riders it was time to say goodbye to Cormack now, and each one did. One by one, they went to the tack room as the vet prepared two large needles full of light-green liquid (one drug was a tranquillizer, and the other was to stop Cormack's heart) in the cold cement hallway. Cormack lay still as the first needle went into his hip, and his eyes closed. After the second needle he let out a little sigh (from both ends) and soon it was over.

"Let's have a wake for Cormack," I said to the riders waiting in the tack room.

"And let's plan how to decorate his grave," said Heather.

"Next week, let's choose him a stone," said another. And before long, we were planning our next Saanich Fair stall decoration entry. Today, a granite boulder marks the spot where Cormack O'Connor lies.

Sometimes I miss those horsey Saanich Fair days with all the little girls—the organizing, the packing, the anticipation! So this year I've decided to go back with Valnah, the Russian woolly horse, just for old times' sake. They still have an award for best stall decorating, and I've designed his stall on a Russian theme—red and gold onion domes and burgundy sashes with shiny tassels. I'll ride too, and hope that the judge likes his movement! I may even go on the tilt-a-whirl in between my classes.

maintaining an outhouse

A GOOD OUTHOUSE WILL HELP you save water and will always be available for use if your plumbing fails. It's a good idea to be as independent as you can be from both technology and government services, just in case.

Here are some tips on maintaining your outhouse:

1. Dig a hole at least six feet deep a good way away from your well. (Check the regulations in your area to get the minimum distance.) Your outhouse should be in a drained area, so that it won't fill up with water during a rainstorm.

2. Make your outhouse attractive: more people will use it if it looks pretty. On Glamorgan Farm, the outhouse is a shake-and-shingle structure with a red tin roof that matches the 10 barns on the farm. The door has a wooden handle, and a blue ceramic moon hangs under the small window. I mow the path right up to the entrance, and a blue

pot of primroses sits beside the door. Last spring I nailed up a birdhouse under the peaked roof, and this year I added a butterfly house.

3. Keep the inside of your outhouse clean and free of slugs (the chickens love them), but leave a few cobwebs to keep the flies under control. Sweep it out regularly. Have lots of toilet paper inside, and a magazine or two. *Gourmet, Martha Stewart's Living* and Oprah's magazine *O* all work well in an outhouse. Hang a calendar on the wall, and if you are expecting guests, pick a bouquet of bluebells and put them beside the seat.

4. To discourage odours and keep things as dry as possible, sprinkle chlorinated lime down the hole daily if your outhouse is in regular use. DO NOT SPILL ANY LIME ON THE SEAT! You will be sorry!

5. Don't use chemical air fresheners in your outhouse—they will prevent nature's microbes from going to work; have a window that opens in your outhouse instead. A healthy outhouse doesn't smell: it perks. The microbes are happy. Think of your outhouse as a giant intestine, busy breaking down bacteria, creating heat and energy, and working in harmony with nature, like a compost pile.

6. If the hole becomes saturated or full, fill it in and move your outhouse to a new location. Throw some wildflowers over the old hole, and you will have a beautiful spot to sit for years to come.

On a hot June day, Glamorgan Farm hosted an old-fashioned Heritage Farm Day. We put a sign up next to the porta-potty that read, "To Outhouse—no Line-up," and we had placed a small bouquet of blue bachelor buttons beside the seat. Many people attended, some dressed up in historic costumes. I saw a lady in a wide, pink, hooped skirt trying to enter the outhouse—she had to toss her ice-cream cone aside into the thistles and overgrown nettle patch to lift her skirt into the tiny structure.

Once a week one summer, city children from the SPCA summer camp came out to spend the day with the farm animals. They had a genuine country experience by also using the outhouse, and at the end of the day were at ease enough not to shriek at the spiders they saw watching them.

The Victoria Sketch Club also came out to visit the farm. They set up their little easels and palettes amongst the poppies in the rockeries, and in nooks and shrubbery around the farm, and I spotted them using the outhouse too.

the ferry dance

DAD LOVES HIS FISHING CAMP on New Brunswick's Miramachi River. He shares it with a few Fredericton lawyers, and they call it the G & G—Grilse and Grouse. They have a salmon smokehouse and a red canoe tied to the shore. Their cottage is nice, quite modern, with a wood stove and lots of stacked-up wood.

One of the lawyers donated a pair of beige recliners, and someone else made some rustic bookshelves that are full of sports magazines. On the wall somebody has hung a fishing-fly display, except all of the flies have silly names; I can picture Dad and his cronies coming up with these at the end of the day, as they were sitting around drinking Scotch and eating pretzels, their hip waders already hung on the porch and a row of silver-blue, pink-tinged fish lined up on the counter ready to fillet. Dad also catches little golden bass on the Saint John River—he calls his favourite spot "the bass hole."

In the summer, Dad goes up to his fishing camp for days at a time and Mum and I always talk on the phone a lot when he's gone. One particularly hot and humid late July, I thought she sounded down. Her days consisted of sleeping and listening to the CBC, she said; she wasn't really seeing many people.

"Bruno doesn't want me to be alone when he goes fishing," she told me one morning. "He wants me to get a girl in. How ridiculous!"

She sounded so morose, I suddenly had an idea. "Why don't you come and spend August with me?" I said.

And Mum said, "Could I?"

Later that day, I went to Sidney and bought Mum an air ticket. She doesn't like to fly alone anymore, so my ex-husband, John, agreed to fly out and get her. They've been the best of friends ever since John accompanied Mum on a trip to Europe years ago. She'd been commissioned by a man in Montreal to paint the tennis matches at Wimbledon and the French Open, and she'd taken John along as her escort.

I went to meet Mum and John at Victoria airport a week later, on a clear, sunny afternoon. As usual, I took along my dogs, and this time I had chubby Ruby, John's dog, as well. I waited in the newly renovated terminal, which is all light and high and airy with a coffee bar at one end and sofas in a circle around some indoor trees. Beyond the runway, through the tall glass windows, I could see the red tin roofs of Glamorgan Farm among the trees and, past those, the sea.

The plane was right on time. Near the end of the crowd disembarking came John in his white T-shirt and blue jeans, carrying the black briefcase I gave him for Christmas about 20 years ago, arm in arm with Mum, who looked small and frail but was smiling. She wore a blue Norwegian sweater and dark glasses to protect her eyes from the light.

"What a long flight," she said in relief as we hugged. "I'm dying to see the dogs."

I took her arm and John, his mission accomplished, trailed along behind happily as we went out into the sun. In the parking lot, the dogs all had their noses pressed against the windows. Mum got into the back seat with Daisy and Lily, because the light wasn't as bright back there.

"How's Dad?" I asked as we turned onto the West Saanich Road. As we drove past the Institute of Ocean Sciences, we could see the red-and-white Coast Guard boats lined up in Pat Bay. The dry, golden meadows of the airport sloped up toward the end of the runway.

"He's fishing," said Mum. "I don't think I even left him a note."

We turned right on Mills Road at the shake-and-shingle heritage church, which is surrounded by shady Garry oaks and wild daisies.

"Oh, there's the little graveyard," Mum said. "There's Freddy and Peggy." Freddy and Peggy had been old friends of Mum's from Saanich.

"And Malcolm," I added, referring to my friend Patsy's late husband.

"Oh, I remember Malcolm," Mum said, recalling him from a painting class she'd given years earlier in my barn. "He loved doing that dot exercise."

We drove up the hill and turned left at the Legion onto Glamorgan Road. "There's that messy place," Mum said as we passed a stucco house with an unmowed lawn littered with old cars and boat engines.

When we got to the farm, John and Ruby left right away in their pickup to catch the last ferry to Galiano. I gave Mum a drink and sat her in a shady spot on the lawn next to a cage full of fat white meat chickens. She took her shoes off and drank, and the meat birds pecked in the grass at their grain. I bring them up onto the porch at night because they can't take the summer night chills. They can't stay in the barn, either, because the rats will attack them.

Mum was tired after her long flight. I outlined for her all the events I had planned for the rest of our summer—won ton soup in Chinatown, dog walks on the beach, a wander through the University of Victoria gardens. "Oh," she sighed, "I'm not up for much. We'll see. And I must remember to call Bruno in a day or two."

For supper, we had chicken soup on the deck and some cherry tomatoes sprinkled with fresh basil I had picked from the HEARTS garden at the front of the property. When it got cool, we went indoors and watched a rerun of *The Royal Canadian Air Farce*. Then Mum went upstairs for her bath.

I puttered around doing dishes, then went outside to close up the farm for the night. I brought in the chicks, locked in the hens and ducks, gave the horses their apples and checked all the gates. When that was done I turned in, snuggling blissfully under my duvet with the evening breeze blowing into my bedroom.

I woke up early and set the table for breakfast, getting out the little yellow teapot with blue polka dots for Mum's tea. While Mum was waking up, I did the outdoor morning chores. As I was coming out of the barn, I saw her amble slowly down the gravel driveway, followed by the dogs, to get the paper.

"I wonder what Bruno is doing today," Mum said during breakfast. "I should call him." We looked at the newspaper and then did our ablutions.

It was a hot day with a clear, blue sky. Mum grabbed the clippers and we strolled around the farm cutting thistles and burdocks. We looked at the pigs and sat on the lawn. I gave Mum a vermouth and she had more chicken soup and then a nap upstairs. When she woke up, I loaded the dogs into the van, put Mum in the front seat and drove us all to Island View Beach, a beautiful stretch of waterfront, with sand and smooth grey stones. Mum was wearing her bathing suit with a pair of shorts over top.

The dogs leapt out as soon as we got there, and Baby Alice Mary was soon floating in the sea like a happy seal. The other dogs ran up and down the beach like excited children. Mum and I walked along the sand to a secluded area, where we sat down on a log.

"I'm cold," Mum said. "I don't feel like a swim anymore."

I drove the scenic way home, through the back roads of North Saanich. That evening we picked rhubarb, cauliflowers and tender broccoli shoots. We blanched and packaged them in plastic bags for the freezer. We picked apples and made applesauce, and then we watched the news before bed.

Our activities on Day Two were just as gentle. After breakfast we wandered down into the HEARTS plots and picked some purple and red dahlias for the living room, some big yellow sunflowers and some fresh basil.

"I should really make pesto," said Mum when we got back to the house, "but I just don't have the energy. I could make some bread, I guess, but what an effort."

I suggested a dog walk at my favourite romp, Blue Heron Park. I got Daisy and Lily and Baby Alice Mary into the van while Mum changed her glasses and put on her sweater. The park has a grassy field to walk across, usually used for children's soccer or baseball. It was filled with a variety of dogs, all cavorting in excitement. Their owners stood chatting in small groups, holding leashes and plastic bags for the inevitable, or threw balls to their pets using racket-type contraptions.

"Oh," Mum said, "this is so west coast. You would never see this in Fredericton. B.C. knows how to have fun."

On our way to the meadow and trails we passed a public toilet with an endearing design. The cement structure is embedded with oyster shells and engravings of swimming fish. That's what I love about North Saanich—quirky surprises like artistic outhouses, and benches in the woods carved by a local First Nations elder from a tree that blew down in a winter storm.

The next morning I went to lift weights at the gym in Sidney. I don't like to go to the gym, but I like the results, and it was part of a program I had designed to lift my spirits. I knew Mum would say, "How ridiculous—you do all that lifting on the farm all day," so I lied and told her that I had won some sessions at the gym and couldn't sell them to anybody else.

Mum insisted on coming along, and she sat at a table beside the chest-press machine while I "worked out." On our way home, we stopped at the video store and rented *Howard's End.* "I wonder what Bruno is doing," Mum said over lunch. "I really should give him a call."

The next day, we decided to go into Victoria for won ton soup in Chinatown. We love the soup at a certain restaurant; it is full of green leafy vegetables, chunks of mushrooms, carrot slices, shrimp and chicken dumplings, and lovely won tons in their soft rice dough. The soup has been the same price—$10—for 20 years. And you get free Chinese tea and a fortune cookie along with it.

After the soup we meandered down the street. Mum said, "I should take something back for Bruno. Not that he deserves anything," she added, but she bought a green ceramic jar of ginger, an item you can't get in Fredericton. Then we strolled along the harbour front, because I wanted Mum to see the Harbour Ferry Ballet.

Every day at 11:45 in Victoria's Inner Harbour, the little green-and-yellow ferries that take people to and from different harbour locations gather to perform a choreographed routine to the tune of "The Blue Danube." The boats are driven by affable retired captains and navy men who dress in white pants and blue blazers. It's an event of true humour, corniness and charm. Mum and I agreed you could almost see the little fat ferries waltzing on their tiptoes. We laughed again about it that night over our scrambled eggs.

I had a surprise for Mum that evening. She had always told me how she loved the Russian film *The Battleship Potemkin*, so I had sent away for it. I thought we could watch it as a good end to the day. But when I asked her, "Would you like to see the movie?" she said, "Not really. Maybe I should phone Bruno to see how he is."

Dad was home from his fishing camp and just going to bed when she reached him. I heard Mum ask how Ernie, their cat, was. Then she asked, "How's the garden?" and "How was the fishing?" When she hung up, she said, "I think I'll go home soon. Bruno misses me." We agreed I'd take her back the next week, the earliest we'd be able to get tickets. Mum went up to her room early that evening. She seemed happy. I headed up the stairs contentedly myself after doing my nightly chores. Autumn was coming—I could smell it in the cool air.

A few days later, a friend of mine called to offer to take Mum and me to Victoria's annual Symphony Splash. We decided to make it our final outing. The Symphony Splash is a grand event in which the Victoria Symphony plays on a barge anchored in the Inner Harbour. It concludes with a brilliant display of fireworks to stirring music. Thousands of people line the upper and lower walkways along the harbour, and hundreds of boats—motorboats, sailboats, dinghies, canoes and kayaks—collect in a compact flotilla of yellows and reds.

We attended the event in my friend's canoe. Mum sat in the middle, wrapped in blankets, and my friend gave her a glass of his pear wine. The sun was going down after another bright, hot day, leaving the sky dusky with shades of yellow and mauve. On our journey from the Victoria Rowing Club docks to the harbour, we passed rusted barges, fishing boats, warehouses and a motionless blue heron perched on a creosoted piling beside an industrial yard heaped with scrap iron and crushed cars. It looked quite beautiful, this pile of metal that had come from the earth, as we paddled quietly through the black water in our old wooden canoe.

Mum sipped her pear wine in time to Brahms' *Hungarian Dances*. The conductor, in his white jacket, waved his arms under the rising moon.

"Oh, I love Brahms," Mum said as she closed her eyes, and soon we were paddling back to the docks so we could get an early start for the airport the next morning.

the smell of home

BECAUSE MUM DOESN'T LIKE TO travel alone anymore, I often take her home to Fredericton after she visits me on the farm. It's a long day to fly across Canada—we leave Glamorgan Farm at dawn and arrive at the Fredericton airport close to midnight. I always look forward to the long hours of nothing to do on the plane but think and read. And usually I stay with Mum and Dad for a couple of days before I fly back home.

The flight down to the Maritimes through the eastern gusts is usually bumpy. The small terminal always has a few people standing in the window under the fluorescent lights, waiting to meet their friends and family. We pass one security guard as we traipse tiredly in, usually an older man. Dad waits for us on a beige vinyl seat inside, because he has gout.

We drive back to the house along dark Lincoln Road. Mum always asks how the cat is, and when we go past the Princess Margaret

Bridge, which crosses the Saint John River, she says, "I wonder how high the river is?"

I lug our bags into the house and, even though it's late, we all sit for a while in the living room and have a drink. Dad always has a can of salted nuts out, but he'll usually offer to make me a fried egg and cheese sandwich. The bedroom I sleep in during my visits has an old spool bed and lots of photographs of me with my animals, which I have sent over the years. Dad's flowering plants fill the deep window-sill. In daylight, the view is of a street lined with elm trees and nicely painted wooden houses.

On one recent visit, on the first morning, Mum and I decided to walk to the grocery store for some provisions. Dad also wanted us to pick up his medication for gout. He stayed home to putter around, watering his plants and sorting his seeds, and then to paint upstairs in the spare room where he has made a studio. Just as we were leaving, he called, "And get a nice cheese for John and Stephen, or a pâté." John and Stephen were friends we were driving out to see at their summer cabin on Harvey Lake that afternoon.

Mum and I walked slowly along Landsdowne Street, past the historic, wooden Loyalist homes with their pretty gardens. We crossed the road at University Avenue and cut through the Beaverbrook rink parking lot. I'd spent my childhood skating at that arena. We walked along railway tracks lined with wild goldenrod, pink clover and fireweed, then crossed a baseball park where, in elementary school, I had once won the provincial high jump.

When we got back, Dad was making lunch, slicing a few pickles, emptying a jar of herring into a blue dish and complaining that the last person to cut the cheese had done it on an angle. After that got sorted out, he asked about his medication. Mum said to me, "Did we get Bruno's gout pills?" and I said, "Yes, they are in your purse." Of course they weren't, but I found them in the grocery bag.

The tension was running a little high by then, so Mum said, "Let's have a vermouth." The three of us sat outside on the wooden steps in the sun and sipped our drinks with ice and a piece of lemon in Mum's green Spanish glasses. I brought out some crackers and a tomato, and soon Dad said, "If we are going to Harvey Lake, we'd better get going."

Harvey is a charming town about 30 miles from Fredericton. Its houses and church and handful of stores are white clapboard with black trim and black shutters. A hand-painted sign in front of the general store read, "Harvey Days This Weekend." John and Stephen's cottage is a dark-blue shake-and-shingle affair with a small lawn in front.

Three weathered Eastern-seaboard deck chairs had been placed around a patch of pansies. Stephen already had the barbecue going and was squirting red sauce on some pork ribs. He seemed energetic, even though he had just come home from a shift at the Fredericton Hospital, where he works on the pediatric ward. Stephen is big and flamboyant with a sweet, kind, happy face and a huge sense of humour. He is younger than John, whom Mum had met years earlier when John worked for the New Brunswick Ministry of Culture.

Part of John's job at the time was to establish the itinerary for Queen Elizabeth's upcoming visit to the province, and he'd asked Mum if she would like to come along to paint it. The queen arrived in a helicopter in a field surrounded by Boy Scouts waving red flags. She disembarked and did a little walk-about wearing a shapeless, powder-blue coat and hat. Mum painted a huge oil of the event and called it *The Queen Comes To New Brunswick.*

John had something wrong with his feet, so he spent his days at Harvey Lake resting while Stephen worked in town. I helped Stephen in the kitchen, and Mum and Dad and John sat out on the deck in a mass of patio furniture, pillows, magazines, citronella candles and ashtrays full of butts. "I'm trying to stop," said John, chuckling. I peeled garlic as Stephen set out a buffet of ribs, corn on the cob, baked potatoes, buns, salads and trout on a white platter. I poured another round of drinks into plastic glasses and carried them outside.

The dinner conversation was hilarious, all about a septic tank that John had tried to help a mutual friend repair on a trip he and Stephen had taken to England. The tank had been clogged with corn kernels and violet toilet paper! Stephen and I sat together with our plates on our laps. As the other three continued talking, we embarked on a profound exchange about what we as people choose to do, or are able to do, with our little lives. We agreed that nobody really cares or pays attention to what you do each day except the day itself. At every moment, even with others around, each of us is really alone. "Whatever we do, only the day will care," Stephen repeated between bites. By that time

I had broken open a jar of red licorice I'd discovered on a small table beside me. I decided the day wouldn't care if I ate the whole thing.

Mum and Dad and I drove back to Fredericton in the charcoal dusk. My flight home was early the next morning, so I rechecked my ticket (for about the tenth time) and then went to bed, full of pasta salad and buns and ribs and licorice. I thought about how much I loved Stephen, and how wonderful it would be if he came to Glamorgan Farm for a week; how I would look after him and show him the sights: the heritage church, the beach, the local bakery, the winery, the Sidney Cinema and our local Polish restaurant.

My trip back across the country was magnificent—smooth flights and sunny all the way. I am often moved to tears when we fly into the little airport in North Saanich after I have been away, but this time, as we taxied toward the new glass terminal surrounded by cows grazing in pastures, and those dark hills in the distance beyond the glinting sea, I felt more of a sense of contentment. Whenever I descend the plane's narrow staircase onto the tarmac, I know I am home because of the familiar smell: that lovely combination of rain, the protected yew trees near the airport and the sea. How I yearned to see the Old Gals, Alice Mary, the cats, and Mabel and Matilda. I was in the burgundy airport taxi in a minute.

gavin's list

ONE OF THE THINGS I like best about going away from Glamorgan Farm is coming back home. If I have been far away, or gone for a long time, I get a surge of "home emotion" as the small plane from Vancouver comes out of the haze of clouds and I see the dark-green Gulf Islands below, patchworked with square, straw-coloured clearings. From up above, you can see every bay and curve of the shoreline and the tiny white surf marks made by fishing boats. Sometimes you can see puffs of smoke coming from the land below.

As we get closer, the plane circles over the pastures of North Saanich, the farms and winding roads between the wineries and garden nurseries, the clusters of rural neighbourhoods separated by hedgerows, trails and gravel lanes. We swoop back out over Pat Bay, where I swim in the summer or take the dogs for a run, and as we descend I can always see the red Coast Guard boats tied up at their dock and the blue pottery shop on the West Saanich Road. If it's nighttime, nearby Sidney glows red and amber across the highway. Once I have a hot bath I call Mum to tell her I am home safely, and if it's dusk I'll walk around the property and inspect.

No matter how good a time I am having, I'm never able to relax completely while I'm away. I worry that the old Appaloosa horse, Duke, will pick the time I'm gone to die, from a stomach ailment or a heart attack or his old creaking hipbones giving out. I worry that a rat will bite the head off a baby duckling, or that there will be a chimney fire in the wood stove, or that one of the cats will be accidentally locked out of the house for the night, or that the septic tank will back up because the friend staying in the house put coffee grounds down the drain or killed the little microbes by using hair dye, or that raccoons will get into the chicken barn, or that a cold spell will descend and my geraniums and pipes will freeze.

Mabel and Matilda, the piggies, might miss their daily scratches and apples, or a windstorm might come up in the night and take off part of the red tin roof. What if the weather while I am away was a combination of sun and warmth and rain? Then the lawn will have grown uncontrollably and my mower will never get through it.

Although I know I'll still have some worries, I try to address most of them by writing up a detailed list before every trip for Gavin, Glamorgan Farm's herb gardener. Even if I have a house-sitter for part of the time, it's Gavin who really takes care of things while I'm gone. For a typical trip, his list may look like this:

Gavin's List: From Anny

I will be at: _____ in _____ from _____ to _____.

If the plane crashes, please call Lorna or Patsy and ask them to make sure that the dogs and cats all stay together on the farm. They'll need somebody to take care of them—there's money for that in the farm account.

You can sell the goats.

People to call in emergencies

Fred Poulson: He has a bulldozer and a digger (in case Duke dies).

Nikki and Norman and White House Stables: They know all about ill livestock.

Bob: He lives at the Sandown racetrack and can fix anything.

John (my ex-husband): He could offer advice and possibly help in some ways.

Mike Walden: My lawyer—he has my will.

chores

DOGS AND CATS · Daisy and Lily, because they are old, need to get outside at dawn, or as early as possible, to relieve themselves.

There are eight cats, Gavin. Little Bee needs to be lifted onto the counter because she has bad arthritis and can't jump up. Give her hard food plus canned. She needs the white powder on the counter sprinkled on her canned food, because she has bad kidneys. Annabelle, the barn cat, should eat on the porch—she can't come in because she fights with the others. Miss Kitty likes to eat slowly and alone, so please feed her at one end of the counter. Jimmy will take everyone's food, so give him extra. Willy, the old ginger cat, is a little odd—he likes to eat some of his food and then go to the bathtub and drink from the tap, so please turn on the tap to a steady drip. He'll return for his food, but maybe stare into space for a while first. (We think he came from a drug house.) Please make sure that Sweet, Pudge and Peter get their fair share.

When the cats have finished, please put all their dishes up on the windowsill, or else Alice Mary will get the dishes off the counter and eat everything that is left.

Clean cat litter boxes every morning. (Even though they can get out the cat door, Willy and Peter prefer to use their litter boxes because of their age.) Because the litter is pine-based, the soiled material can go on the burn pile out behind the outhouse when you change it.

When Lily and Daisy come in, feed Lily in the pantry. She likes cooked carrots, which are in the fridge. Daisy will eat under the kitchen table—she likes her food on the floor, not in a dish. Feed Baby Alice Mary in the porch or she will take the others' food, because she finishes so fast. She might go down to the racetrack after breakfast to get a treat from Bob, who lives in a trailer there, so don't worry if she disappears.

By the way, Annabelle the cat likes eggs, and the dogs can each have one too, about every three days.

BIRDS IN LIVING ROOM · Homer and Virgil are the finches in one cage, and Pip is the canary in the other. One of the finches has only one leg—don't be alarmed! He got that injury years ago and copes very well.

The birds need fresh water and grain every day. Every other day they can have a piece of apple or broccoli, but it has to be organic—they won't touch it otherwise. You can pick the broccoli from the Healthy Harvest garden—they have a plot of the Italian purple sprouting variety—and you can pick the apples from the trees in the hedgerow. The birds like the apple seeds, too. Cut the apples into quarters.

Also, the birds really love fresh branches of apple blossom, Indian plum, honeysuckle or saskatoon berry, which you can pick from the Sandown woods. The clippers are by the woodpile. Don't pick the hawthorn. My Gran always told me it was very bad luck to bring hawthorn into the house!

If you have time, please pick up a few (clean) chicken feathers from the henhouse floor and put them in the birds' cages. They will use them to line their nests.

PIGGIES · Mabel and Matilda can pretty much look after themselves, but they would love a back scratch every day with the metal curry comb and, if you are up to it, each of them can have an apple, too.

If it's really hot, please turn on the sprinkler in their pen—it will make mud that they can lie in to cool their skin, and will also give them a shower. They don't have sweat glands, except in their snouts, so they like to be kept cool.

The pigs get sow kibble twice a day, and for a treat they can have a (big) handful of alfalfa at noon. Because they like it for sleeping, please throw several flakes of hay into their beds every two days. I cooked them some yams and potatoes, and you can add that to their feed. It's in the fridge next to Lily's cooked carrots.

If the rat exterminator comes, please tell him to set a trap in the piggie barn. Yesterday I saw two large fat rats eating Mabel's parsnip.

HORSES · The horses are shedding. Use the curry comb or the shedding blade and comb their coats in long, straight strokes. Leave the hair outdoors so that the wild birds can pick it up for their nests. The barn swallows like it especially.

Duke is old and slow and stiff. He is losing his sight and his hearing, so be patient with him. He should have a warm molasses bran mash every five days to keep his insides cleaned out, especially if it rains and he's cold, in which case he should also stay in at night with a blanket thrown over his hips. I've left separate instructions on how to make the bran mash, in case you've forgotten.

Fred Ball will come up and trim the horses' hooves if they get too long. He will cut up the hoof clippings, and you'll notice that the dogs will pick them up and chew on them. The toenails contain some glutinous material they just love.

If the horses get too much mud in their hooves, clean it out with a pick. Then brush off the hoof, especially in the cracks, with a stiff brush, and pour in a few drops of the green copper liquid. This will prevent hoof rot (thrush).

Duke likes his face rubbed with a damp cloth, especially around the eyes, and Valnah likes his elbows rubbed hard every day with a stiff curry comb (his wool makes him itchy).

GOATS · Pearl and Princess get fed twice a day. Most of the time they like to sit up on their rocks. You can let them out, but watch that they don't go down to the allotment gardens. Just open their gate and they'll dart out and follow you around the farm.

They love the poplar leaves. They like carrot peelings and broccoli, if it's cut up into bite-sized pieces, and they like bread, too. They are quite naughty, especially Pearl (the larger white one), so keep an eye on them. To get them back in their pen, just get a little of their grain and shake the can.

CHICKENS · Mix, in the big red tub, five cans of cracked corn, five cans of Lay Crumbles and five cans of Scratch, then throw this out into their pen.

Some chickens, such as the Polish Crested (they lay the white eggs), like their grain indoors, and the red dwarf hen, Little Lydia, needs to have a handful given to her in her box, because she's too old to go out. They can have food scraps and compost as well, but they can't stand onions or oranges.

Every morning, change the water in their yellow water buckets. They also like fresh hay in their laying boxes every other day.

There are rats in the henhouse. They dig up from under the floor and make huge piles of earth, but they don't seem to bother the chickens. Sometimes you might find a dead rat floating in their water, though.

Don't forget to collect the eggs!

DUCKS · Jewel is sitting on one egg in the duckhouse, so you may not see much of her. She's determined to hatch this one.

Please change their pool water every day. I have left some bread for them in the barn. Little Jessica and Jemima like worms, so if you have time, can you just turn over the soil for a few moments here and there? Jake the Drake won't go in at night on his own, so you have to push him with the rake.

If the duckling hatches when I am gone, please make sure that he or she has a shallow pan to drink from. Use the baking pan from the stove drawer.

Thanks, Gavin! Good luck. If I remember anything else, I'll leave a note on the kitchen table.

by the dawn's early light...

i: the frankfurter

NEW YORK WAS ONE OF those places I had always wanted to visit.
I had heard all about the bagels, Central Park, the Staten Island ferry,
the skyscrapers, the neon signs beaming along Broadway and high-
end shops such as Bloomingdale's, Saks and Macy's. I had a vision of
myself standing on the sidewalk beside the steam gushing up from a
manhole, eating a frankfurter amongst the honking yellow cabs.

I've been a councillor in North Saanich for the past two terms,
and last spring, while I was the acting mayor, an opportunity came
up to go to the Big Apple. The global organization Mayors for Peace
was sponsoring a conference at the United Nations, in memory of the
bombing of Hiroshima, to discuss nuclear disarmament.

I packed up a load of brass North Saanich pins and small Canadian
flags and persuaded my friend Maureen to accompany me. We took a

midnight flight from Vancouver, via Toronto, to La Guardia Airport. In the grey light of early dawn, our jet dipped out of the clouds and did a graceful turn over Manhattan. The sight below took my breath away—an array of beautiful towers, all different heights and shapes, some glimmering gold, some silver, some looking like wedding cakes, some with spires and some in clusters that resembled a set of pastels standing upright. And there, tiny, was the Statue of Liberty in the dark water.

Maureen and I took a yellow cab downtown. We were supposed to participate in the Mayors for Peace march at noon, then attend the rally in Central Park at a baseball diamond. The taxi pulled up on 51st Street in front of a windblown awning reading "The Pickwick Arms." Maureen had boasted that her sister-in-law knew all about New York and had told her "The Pickwick Arms is fabulous—it's where all the artists stay." (Maureen later confessed over a glass of wine that her sister-in-law had actually said, "It's where all the *starving* artists stay.") The lobby was small with a few faded, maroon, upholstered chairs and a brass plaque above a gas fireplace.

Our room was tiny. Its two single beds, with brown polyester covers, were separated by an arborite stool and a flickering fluorescent lamp. Our view was another yellow-brick building 10 feet away. Maureen called the buildings "brownstones" and took a picture. While she went into the bathroom "to put on her face," I looked at the map. I thought we could pick up the mayors' march at 56th Street and Madison if we walked up and over a few blocks.

It was a sunny day in New York. As we left the hotel we saw a group of protesters at the Singapore embassy across the street. Next door to the Pickwick Arms was an elegant-looking wine bar, and farther down the block we passed a filthy neon sign chained to an iron gate that led down some gritty stairs, which read, "Psychic—let Claudia guide you toward love, money and happiness—$5.00 a reading." The sign was switched off at the moment, but Maureen and I decided to see Claudia for a laugh after the march and to visit the wine bar, too.

We set off toward Central Park, where the march was scheduled to end up, passing Indian restaurants, gleaming smoked-glass banks and corner flower stalls filled with buckets of roses, lilies, lilacs and freesias. Maureen, star-struck, gasped, "Oh my god, it's Bloomingdale's!" And then a few minutes later, "Oh my god, it's the Trump building!" and then, "Park Avenue!" Finally we saw the edge of the park, a wonderful blend of pale-pink plum blossoms and soft green leaves. Horses and carriages were lined up on the street, and hot-dog and pretzel vendors stood on every corner.

I said to Maureen, "I have to have a frankfurter in New York!" She took my picture holding a plain hot dog with a yellow squirt of mustard. Her camera jammed, though, and she had to repeat the picture. I was getting a bit embarrassed—I wanted to be a New Yorker, detached and cool and rich in culture, and instead I was holding a wiener as Maureen was saying, "Smile!" in front of tons of real New Yorkers rushing by.

Somehow we had missed the march, so we kept walking and finally asked a policeman standing under a willow tree where the global peace rally was. We were close, as it turned out; it was just around the pond. We got to the baseball diamond as the marchers were arriving, so we pulled out our Canadian flags and joined in.

As the people gathered into a huge peace symbol, Maureen and I sat down under a shady tree. It was humid; you could almost see steam rising from the baseball mounds. A rock band was playing, and casual police stood around the field with their thumbs in their belt loops.

A few tables had been set up to sell buttons and T-shirts. Maureen bought me a bumper sticker that read "Well-behaved Women Rarely Make History." While she filled her bag with pamphlets and chatted to like-minded people about the American version of the Green Party, I ate a cheese-filled pretzel that hit my stomach hard. When Maureen returned, she was wearing an army cap in camouflage colours that had a peace symbol on the front.

The sun was going down as we strolled out of the park. Maureen, who knows everything about high-end shopping, saw a sign across the road for Barneys. "Barneys is the top!" she said excitedly. We crossed the street, politely waiting for the Walk sign even though everybody else walked, and gazed at Barneys' windows. The mannequins were bronzed and sinewy, in reclining positions. For some reason, none of them had heads. Maureen particularly admired a pair of men's powder-blue shorts with a luxurious leather belt.

We wandered slowly back toward the hotel, taking in the sights and sounds around us. As we were crossing Lexington Avenue, Maureen spotted a very elegant man in a pin-striped suit and pink silk tie walking a corgi. Since she breeds and shows corgis at home, she said to him excitedly, "That's a lovely corgi." Like a typical New Yorker, he ignored her. I've never confessed to Maureen that her corgi, Shorty, bit me and drew blood out on her driveway one summer evening when I'd been invited to her house for dinner.

The wine bar beside our hotel turned out to be very French, very soothing and very private. The waitresses were sweet young women from Paris in tight black miniskirts and red blouses with welcoming smiles. Our wine was served in globe glasses, round thin glasses with long stems. Maureen and I vowed to buy some globe glasses in Sidney when we got home, and some good wine, too. We ordered raw oysters and eggplant pâté and more wine, and then I suggested we visit Claudia, the psychic down the block. Maureen agreed to go first.

"If you're not back in 15 minutes, I'll come and find you," I promised.

A jazz band had begun to play in the corner of the bar, and men and women in business suits were drifting in. Maureen returned after about 10 minutes, looking shaken.

"She's good," said Maureen. "I only had my palm read. She did make one mistake, though—she thought I was a writer."

Now it was my turn. "I might be longer," I warned Maureen. I intended to go for the full psychic reading.

Claudia was a well-groomed dark woman wearing a stretchy orange top. I sat down in a red velvet chair beside a round table covered in a gold tablecloth as she explained her services. Palms for $5, crystal cleansing for $20, Tarot cards and teacups for $25. When I selected the psychic reading for $30, she handed me a pad and said to write down my name and birth date. The letterhead on the pad read "Howard's Window Washing."

Once she had that information, Claudia went into a sort of trance. "You will have a long life," she said in a dreamy voice. She had a vaguely Italian accent. "Your mother will be ill soon but will recover—don't worry. You will move by the end of the year. It will be a good move, and the person who loves you is torn." She paused. "However," she continued, "you have negative forces inside you that are blocking you from the success you deserve. Your book should have been on the bestseller list by now."

That blew me away. Maybe in Smithers, I thought.

Claudia stopped abruptly. "I can cleanse you of this negative energy, and you will find peace and happiness and success. It will have to be tomorrow though. Oprah comes on in 10 minutes, and she's interviewing Tom Cruise today. But I will do a meditation for you tonight to locate these evil spirits. Come tomorrow. For $30 more I will tell you what I find."

Maureen and I went to a seafood café on Second Avenue for dinner. I ordered swordfish and Maureen had cod, and we shared a piece of New York cheesecake for dessert. At one point we were sure we'd spotted a famous actress in the café, but we couldn't think who it was. Back in the wine bar, the jazz band was winding down as the dark New York midnight deepened. We were quite content as we made our way upstairs to our tiny beds and grungy room.

ii: the little way

The next morning Maureen and I decided to visit St. Patrick's Cathedral, the Gothic architectural marvel in the heart of midtown Manhattan. We had breakfast first at a local café with a yellowed sign pasted in the window which read "Oatmeal served All Day." The oatmeal must be to serve the local Scots, and I thought it was for the older population.

The cathedral was very calming and beautiful. I went from marble alcove to marble alcove, reading about all the saints. The white silk banners, the elaborate, polished, silver candlesticks, the smell of incense and the glow of beeswax on the pews made me ache to be a believer—what a place this would be in which to pray.

My favourite saint of the group was Saint Theresa, the Little Flower. Her sign said that her mother had died when she was an infant and that she had become a nun and kept a diary and loved gardening and flowers, especially roses. According to the description, Theresa did good works and expected nothing in life, and she died very young. In her diary, Theresa had written that she would follow her "little way" to her purpose. I fell in love with her when I read that she was full of self-doubt. I lit a candle for her and put a dollar in the box. She also suffered from indigestion, said the sign. Theresa and I had a lot in common.

By the time Maureen and I went out through the cathedral's carved-oak doors into the bright sunlight I had to go to my appointment with the psychic. Maureen went off to get tickets for some Broadway shows.

Claudia's door was open so I knocked, and then went in. She was busy spraying the room with peach air freshener. The TV was on, tuned to *The Ellen DeGeneres Show*.

"I did the meditation," Claudia said solemnly once we were settled. She began to concentrate, almost tremble. I could hear Ellen telling her audience that they were all going to get some chocolates for attending. "You are a reincarnated person," Claudia said. "You were a leader, hated by some, and you died much too soon, from a fall—no, a blow to the head." She came out of her trance and asked me sharply, "Are you afraid of falling?"

I said, "Well, um, yes, I suppose I am," because I didn't want to hurt her feelings.

Next Claudia rubbed pink crystal stones all over me and said a chant to rid me of demons. I noticed that one of the stones had a crack in it and was stuck together with Scotch tape.

"This is what I want you to do," she said, very seriously. "Right now, go and buy a banana. It is the fruit of goodness, and it will bring you joy and growth. Then buy one red rose, which will bring love into your life." Then came the clincher: "Go to the bank and bring me $2,500, which will bring you power." Claudia opened her door. "Go now. Come back immediately, and don't tell anyone, or the spell will not work."

I went back to the hotel to tell Maureen. We decided to go to the wine bar for lunch.

"Take her one dollar," Maureen advised over our salads, "and tell her that should symbolize enough power. Then come right back and we'll go to the Museum of Modern Art."

I ran up to the corner and bought a banana, then stopped at a floral stand and bought a red rose. Claudia was watching *Court TV* when I returned. I explained there was no way I could get $2,500.

"Okay," she sighed. "We'll do it another way, with candles." She rubbed the banana all over me and said some chant about joy, then did the same with the rose and said some chant about love.

"To fully rid you of the negative spirits," she said, "I must light three candles, which will burn for nine days. After that, your life will change. Each candle costs $300, which you must pay today."

"I'll think about it," I said, as I got up to leave.

"You know where I am," she said, glancing over at the TV. "You owe me $60 for today."

Maureen was waiting in the wine bar. She roared with laughter when I told her what had happened and bought me a glass of exquisite French wine. I put the red rose on the table, alongside the banana, then pulled out the little plastic card about Saint Theresa I'd bought that morning. "Little Flower, please pick me a rose from the heavenly garden and send it to me with a message of love," I read aloud.

"Theresa must be taking care of you already," said Maureen.

We saw three exhibitions at the Museum of Modern Art. The first one was an installation about Houdini featuring an empty playpen, a model of a man's hairy legs nailed to the wall and a top hat inside a Plexiglas box with a pair of handcuffs. The next exhibit was similarly mysterious—a line of silvery glass jars on a counter, each labelled with the name of a human excretion: Piss, Pus, Mucous, Saliva, Sweat, Semen and Snot, etc. I noticed there was no jar labelled "tears." The third exhibit, called "Groundswell," consisted of models, slides and illustrations of the new age of urban planning in the major cities of the world. The philosophy was that city centres should be redesigned with parks and art so that they could once again become real town squares. The most touching model was from Beirut. The war-torn city centre had become a green space called "The Garden Of Forgiveness."

That night Maureen and I had supper at an Indian place around the corner. Once we got to bed, neither of us could sleep, because the day had been so stimulating.

"I'm still hungry," Maureen said.

"Have the banana," I suggested.

"Who do you think you were reincarnated from?" Maureen asked as she sat up to peel the fruit.

"A blow to the head, a fall, a leader betrayed ..." I repeated Claudia's words. "Maybe it was Ivan the Terrible's son."

Maureen and I had taken a boat trip along the Volga River a year earlier, and we'd heard the story of how Ivan had struck him down in a rage.

"Maureen?" I said. "Can I have a bite of that banana?"

But Maureen had fallen sound asleep.

iii: coffee with the ambassador

The next day was the Mayors for Peace conference at the United Nations. Maureen and I went back to the "Oatmeal served All Day" place for breakfast, then set out. As we walked, the scene gradually changed from hole-in-the-wall hardware shops displaying mops and colourful sponges on the sidewalk to areas of smooth concrete and smoke-blue skyscrapers.

At an office in the Turkish embassy, we received our conference packages and a UN security card. I had to admit, if to nobody but myself, that I was less than enthusiastic about spending a lovely sunny New York day in a carpeted conference room talking about nuclear disarmament, even if the speaker was Kofi Annan. But Maureen seemed to be enjoying herself as we milled about, chatting to mayors from everywhere from Delhi to Manchester and eating the free cake and muffins. One mayor had his daughter with him; she was carrying a copy of *Teen Magazine* in a pink plastic shopping bag.

The UN complex was surprisingly low-key: several concrete-and-glass buildings fronted by a row of colourful flags. I searched out the maple leaf and there it was, fluttering near the centre. I felt a pang of pride as I stood, holding my new hemp "Mayors for Peace" shoulder bag (which also came with a note pad and a water bottle). I had a handful of the North Saanich pins in my pocket ready to exchange with all the mayors of the world.

When we filed into the great conference room, I got a kick out of seeing Maureen's and my place cards propped up at seats in the back row. "Acting Mayor: Anny Scoones, North Saanchin, Canada," mine said. Beside me was the seat for the mayor of Montreal.

Various speeches followed. I especially liked the affable mayor from Christchurch, New Zealand, who told us, "New Zealand is a nuclear-free country. We have paid the price, and it's a price worth paying." If I ever visited New Zealand, I thought, I would look him up. The mayor of Montreal was passionate, speaking of love and compassion and justice. At one point I felt a tap on my shoulder. A smiling man said, "I'm representing Burnaby, B.C.—want to exchange pins?" And we did.

After the final speech, Maureen and I decided to tour the UN lobby rather than listen to the scheduled lectures. Maureen roamed one display area that depicted the women of the world. Why, I wondered, if the UN was so concerned about women and equality, were there no female judges on the UN Court of Justice? Why were nine out of 10 UN staff men?

Before heading back to the hotel, Maureen and I were invited to meet a man with a very long title—The Ambassador and Permanent

Representative to the United Nations for Disarmament—just a block away. All of the Canadian mayors had been invited.

The ambassador's office had a view of the East River and the UN. Maureen and I were settled at a very large polished wooden table. A secretary offered us coffee, but when we accepted, she had to run out to get it. She returned with a bag from Starbucks. I blurted out, "I boycott Starbucks," as she handed me a cup. Then she realized she'd forgotten to get cream.

Nobody else showed up except a councillor from Vancouver. He talked about how Vancouver was hosting a peace conference soon. Somebody brought in some cream, but by then my coffee was cold. And that was our meeting with the ambassador.

Maureen and I wandered back to the Pickwick Arms lugging our UN shopping bags. I was longing for the wine bar, not so much for the wine, but for a place of neutral ease where those waitresses in their red shirts would bring me little bread slices and I could just drift.

iv: the showman

Maureen and I were scheduled to leave New York the next afternoon. We decided to spend our remaining time in the city by taking a two-hour ferry ride along the Hudson River to see the skyline of New York and the Statue of Liberty. It was corny, but something we had to do.

The day was unsettled—cloudy and windy, with only a few blue patches of sky above the skyscrapers. At the lower end of Manhattan, we saw the gap where the World Trade Center towers had been. Just as we rounded the tip of Manhattan, the boat's showman, who was wearing a stretchy black jumpsuit, began to sing "New York, New York." The music blasted through the speakers outdoors.

Then, looking a weathered green in the grey light, there was the Statue of Liberty. The boat circled around her as we headed back up the Hudson. For a moment, as I stood on the windy deck, I felt I understood what she meant. A new beginning, a fresh chance—hope and a home.

But then the man in the stretchy suit began to sing the American national anthem, ruining everything. Maureen and I went back inside, where the other passengers were piling heaps of New York cheesecake and whipped cream onto their plates. A few hours later, we were at the airport, in the WestJet lineup.

The next morning, very early, Mum called to hear all about New York. The Saint John River was flooding its banks, she said, and Dad was busy moving all the paintings up out of the basement. I was glad to be home.

the contraption

A FEW YEARS AGO, MY friend Lorna and I went to Malaysia. She had been invited to read her poetry at a cultural event during the Commonwealth Games there. When she told me that she would be staying in a five-star hotel, I went along to keep her company.

I flew in a week after Lorna, arriving late at night. From the window of the shuttle bus to the hotel, I could see deep-pink tropical blossoms down the centre of the boulevard. Kuala Lumpur was lit up like a fairyland, with strings of white lights in the trees. Colourful night markets in narrow alleyways were jammed full of red-painted stalls selling silks and watches and spices and exotic fruit. Cafés served steaming soup in white china bowls to customers sitting at tables on the street.

As the bus drove through the busy warmth of the city, I remembered my Auntie Irene, who had married Mum's brother Willoughby, telling us in her extremely British accent about her trip to "Malaya" in the 1930s. She'd met a dentist who took a shine to her and flew her around in his Moth, she said. I'd had to suppress a fit of the giggles at the image of her in a leather cap, goggles and silk scarf, because she was such a proper, church-going lady by then.

The bus pulled up in front of a beige, polished-marble lobby, all lit up with crystal chandeliers. I was a bit bedazzled as I called Lorna from the lobby. Potted palms, deep plush leather couches and fountains welcomed me as I made my way to the gleaming brass elevator.

The next day, after Lorna had been picked up by a black limousine to continue her cultural obligations, I decided to take a walk around town and perhaps visit the jade museum I saw marked on my city map. I passed lots of women on the bustling streets, some in black robes with their faces covered, others in miniskirts and high heels. It was 40 degrees outside under a blazing sun, and the humidity that day was rated at 90 percent.

I was soaked in sticky perspiration by the time I knocked on a red door with the words "Malaysian Jade Museum" painted in dripping green letters on a cardboard sign. A small woman took my money and let me into two dim, cool rooms full of glass cases. In the corner of one room a man in a white undershirt sat watching TV. I looked for a few minutes at the Buddhas and bowls and vases in the cases, then quietly made my way out.

Back at the hotel, Lorna and I lay in shaded lounge chairs beside the hotel pool, and I ordered us some fizzy mint drinks. We had a hilarious time speculating about the people around us.

The next day, we decided to visit the Kuala Lumpur prison, which is now a museum. The grey stone building took up two city blocks. There were rolls of razor wire winding along the top of its walls. The sidewalk outside was crumbling, and rebar protruded from the curb.

Once we got inside, we were shown into a room with hard wooden chairs lined up in front of a large TV set. The guide told us to sit down, and he turned on a video. A stern-looking male soldier in a tailored khaki uniform appeared on the screen, a neat little pistol at his hip. He spoke in English, explaining the rules and laws in Malaysia; any person who disobeyed these laws, even by littering or spitting, would be arrested and put in prison. Lorna and I sat there like bad schoolgirls, watching intently.

When the soldier's spiel was complete, he was replaced on the screen by a female soldier in a tight khaki skirt and knee-high black leather boots. The female soldier carried a long black riding whip. As she warned us against importing drugs to Malaysia, she grinned widely, exposing a row of bright white teeth. "Malaysia does not tolerate drugs, as this prison will show you," she said, bending the tip of the whip slowly back and forth. Lorna and I were mesmerized.

The prison property was immense, but everything was divided up into sections separated by high stone walls. In the middle of one grassy courtyard was a large wooden contraption with bloodstains on the boards and a long leather lash in a holder on the side. The accompanying video showed the device in use: a naked man was strapped onto the boards and then flogged by a woman in uniform. There was no sound on the video, and everything was shown in slow motion. Close-ups of the man's red-streaked buttocks showed his flesh jiggling with every strike.

In a dirty hallway farther on, a yellow Plexiglas shield separated two rows of torn, green vinyl seats. The cells themselves were grim stone boxes with iron doors. On the walls of some we could see number signs, perhaps indicating the days or months that had passed.

The presentation of the death chamber was silly. A dark tunnel led dramatically to a wooden platform, where we stood in front of a noose. Lights flashed in time to a loud recording of the platform giving way. There was another dramatic moment, then silence and darkness. A security guard escorted us through the prison's final hallway.

Outside, in the blazing sun, the traffic was heavy. Lorna and I began to walk, and then the strangest thing happened: we couldn't articulate anything. At one point I tried to say "Let's retrace our footsteps," but I couldn't think of the word for footsteps. Lorna kept saying, "I know the word you mean, but I can't remember it either—'footfall'?" And I had never heard of the word "footfall"—it was if we were stunned. We kept walking in the heat, crossing at the walk lights like robots.

That night we decided we wanted to experience something familiar and secure, so I suggested a nearby hamburger place. It was an outlet of a burger chain that is famous for featuring T-shirts from around the world.

The place was noisy, crowded with men in suits and women in beautiful clothing, all having burgers and beer. Lorna and I ordered, and then, on a napkin, we plotted out an idea that seemed brilliant at the time. It was for a Poet's Museum, which we would set up in the big barn at Glamorgan Farm. We would display Susan Musgrave's decorated car, the pin from Patrick Lane's broken ankle, and other such items. Lorna then created a rare artifact by blotting her lipstick on another napkin from the famous burger chain.

After we'd finished our supper, we took a final walk through the city. The place was spotless and full of activity, a strange mix of the night markets smelling of fish and incense, and big black limousines and skyscrapers. People walked with their heads down, in silence. Perhaps they feared that, if they caused any trouble, they would end up on the flogging contraption.

the lampshade

ABOUT THREE YEARS AGO, I flew to Glasgow for a week's holiday. I had been working hard on Glamorgan Farm and as a municipal councillor, and my Glasgow trip was a quiet, reflective time. I wandered the city, up and around the red-brick buildings that lined the narrow streets, through the roughly kept parks and in amongst the stolid stone buildings of the old university. Glasgow is a rustic city, not a cleaned-up tourist castle town like Edinburgh. It seemed to be a town that knew about struggle—the Moscow of Scotland, not the beautiful, elegant St. Petersburg.

Cities with feelings are interesting. One year Mum and I went to Prague. It was stunning, with its iron bridges and its rivers and its pastel buildings, its parks and Mozart concerts, but as Mum said one night, "Prague is lovely, but I can't find its soul." Glasgow had a soul—I felt it as I meandered through the sooty streets.

On my final day, I decided to visit a section of town called the

Gorbals. According to the map, you could walk a mile east along the river to a museum that focussed specifically on Glasgow history. I set out from my hotel, strolling along a twisting route past many boarded-up buildings. Nothing seemed to be open, and there was almost nobody on the streets, which were littered with cigarette butts and gobs of saliva. It was a lovely morning. The sky was steel grey, with a yellow strip far off on the horizon. A wind was picking up.

The early part of my walk was uneventful. Then two strange things occurred. First, out of nowhere, I came upon a small building with a red-painted door. On the sign that swung from a hinge above it were the words "Russian Café." There was a light on inside. I was excited, because of my inexplicable obsession with Russia, but also a little disappointed that the mysterious country I loved had infiltrated the West. What was a Russian restaurant doing in the dark poor bowels of Glasgow?

I went in, and the place was very modest. I once heard the famous French actress Catherine Deneuve say on TV about Russians, "They are rough, but they are romantic." I think the two go hand in hand. The restaurant had wooden chairs and tables with red table-cloths and candles on them. Cartoon-like pictures of flowers and fairies and dragons hung in cheap plastic frames on the dark yellow walls. I was the only customer, and I ordered a Bloody Mary and some pickles and herring with sour cream from a man with a dark beard. A sombre woman with her hair in a bun was off in a corner doing the accounts.

I continued down the street after my Russian break. When I got to the river, I turned left, as the map indicated. This was a busier street, and a few dirty trucks roared past, smelling of thick, brown diesel. I had to walk through a dimly lit tunnel to get across the river and as I did, a sudden whoosh of diesel air, mixed with the faint smell of urine, rushed through. I looked down and saw an elegant, cream-coloured, silk lampshade with a fringe, rolling along the gutter. I caught it and then continued to walk, holding the lampshade carefully by its top.

The Glasgow History Museum had a gift shop selling books and postcards. The featured exhibit was called "Staircases," a series of pastels by a local artist of the doorways and staircases of the narrow, red-brick, working-class houses that are all over Glasgow—"tenement houses," I think they call them. I sat on a black vinyl bench to admire the pastels and put the fringed lampshade down beside me.

Then I noticed a poem on the wall at the room's entrance:

> *When I was walking up the stair,*
> *I met a man who wasn't there,*
> *He wasn't there again today,*
> *Oh how I wish he'd go away.*

The poem put me in a rather melancholy state, and the lampshade and I walked slowly back to the hotel through the grim streets. I packed my bag, then went down to the restaurant off the lobby to eat some sausages.

After I was finished, I asked the tired-looking woman behind the desk in the lobby if she had any plastic bags and tape I could use to ship home a lampshade. She did, and gave me some twine as well. I wrapped up the shade and had a bath, then went to bed and watched the BBC news. Princess Anne's bull terrier, Florence, had bitten a child in a park. The wound was only a scratch, but the parents were suing.

The Air Canada clerk at the Glasgow Airport next morning wouldn't let me take my lampshade on as hand luggage. "But it's my hat," I said, thinking quickly. "May I carry on my hat?" The answer was still no. I covered the package with Air Canada "Fragile" stickers and sadly watched it go down the chute.

I had to change planes in Toronto and then again in Vancouver, where, before going through Customs, I was made to walk across a wet pink carpet of chemicals to rid my shoes of any Scottish germs. In Victoria, tired at the end of my journey, I stood waiting in a crowd of travellers by the luggage turnstile. I could hardly wait to get home. I kept thinking about my new lampshade, and how it would look on the tarnished brass tripod lamp in my living room.

The luggage from our flight began to appear on the rubber carousel. I grabbed my duffle bag, then watched in dismay as a pile of crumpled green plastic rolled off the chute, "Fragile" stickers twisted in amongst sprung wire, twine and silk fringe.

Late that night, in the warmth of my living room, I gingerly cut the wrapping off my poor lampshade. I felt as if I were dressing a wound. The dogs lay around me, and the embers from the fire glowed.

I had picked a bouquet of quince blossoms as the sun was going down and called Mum to tell her I had returned home safely.

I began to bend the crumpled lampshade back into shape. The silk was torn, and the shade looked much the worse for wear, but, crooked as it was, it did fit on top of the brass pole lamp. The light shone through the silk, and I sat under it for a while and read *Land of the Firebird*, my favourite book by Suzanne Massey, about the cultural history of Russia. When the embers in the fireplace had died down completely, I switched off the lamp and went to bed.

Ever since, when Mum comes to stay, I read to her under the soothing light of that silk shade. She lies on the green sofa by the fire. "Read that part again about Ivan the Terrible's dinner," she says.

scenes from a little life

NOT LONG AGO, I SIGNED up for a trip with the University of Victoria, a cultural excursion to parts of Ontario. We were scheduled to see plays at the Shaw Festival at Niagara-on-the-Lake and at Stratford, where William Hutt was playing Prospero in *The Tempest* in one of his final performances before retirement, as well as to visit some galleries and museums. My friend Maureen decided to join me.

After a turbulent flight, we landed in Toronto, where we boarded a roomy, air-conditioned bus. Lydia, our wonderfully efficient tour guide, announced over the microphone that the bus had a chemical toilet at the back. As we drove along congested Highway 401, she passed around a box of her homemade raisin and orange muffins and a map of our route. The pink wavy line went around the west end of Lake Ontario to Niagara-on-the-Lake. Soon the many lanes of traffic gave way to green fields, small towns with narrow, tree-lined streets and a view of the white-capped lake in the distance.

A few hours later, our bus pulled up in front of a hotel called the Pillar and Post. The lovely, red-brick building was trimmed with fresh black enamel paint, and lush baskets full of pink blossoms swung from the ornate balconies. Maureen and I checked into our plush room, which was done up in a pale yellow, then headed immediately to the spa to see what they offered. I booked a head massage and something for feet called "reflexology." Maureen booked a full massage. Then we went for lunch upstairs and paid $50 for two small Caesar salads.

The first play we saw was *Gypsy*, an afternoon performance of the showy musical with elaborate red, gold and turquoise scene changes at the main Festival Theatre. The actors gave it everything they had. Shoulders smartly back and legs apart, they belted out the tunes, mouths wide open, hands at their sides and fingers flared. I felt very sorry for the desperate stage mother of Gypsy Rose Lee. It was a wonderful story. It nagged me that there really was no resolution to it, but then, that's life—there never is.

That evening, at a smaller theatre on the main street, we saw *Journey's End*, about a group of soldiers in the trenches during World War One. At the end of the play, they go "over the top," and you know they are all going to die. The play made me cry, especially when the actors took their curtain call dressed as soldiers, helmets on, with their pathetic, red-ribboned medals pinned to their chests.

The next day I went for my reflexology session. The room glowed with candles and smelled of eucalyptus. I was lying down on a nice, clean, white bed, but I couldn't relax because I was afraid that the soft-handed beautician would touch a tender nerve in my foot. Sure enough, she did. The pain corresponded to my bladder, she said. Now I was not only $80 poorer, but concerned that I had an infection, even though there was no outward sign of it. After that I couldn't stop worrying about my possible bladder infection.

After lunch I walked into town and rented a bicycle. The streets of Niagara-on-the-Lake are lined with sycamore trees, and the heritage houses have carefully mowed lawns and sometimes polished iron gates or brick pathways. The shops are small and charming, with pretty awnings and signs. The bike shop was down a narrow side street, across from a cigar store and beside a wooden building with a sign that read "The Angel Inn."

The rented bike came with a suggested route and a map. It had a wide, comfortable seat, a roomy carrier basket and a bell. The bike was modern, with many gears and thick rubber tires, and I seemed to glide out of town. My destination was the wineries that line the Niagara River.

I rode past Fort Saint George, a national historic site. In the distance, to my left, was Lake Ontario, looking all fresh and white-capped and glinting in the breeze that had come up. The big shady trees really did filter the sunlight through them, just as the Romantic poets described. I rode a long way along the river, passing some of the big winery estates, and finally turned off onto a country road.

There were more wineries here, on a smaller scale. The first one I entered was quite chic. The wines were elegantly placed on pine shelving, and olive-green gift bags with a gold silk ribbon were included with your purchase. I continued down the road in the brilliant sunshine. After a while, a small farm with a gravel driveway and a tidy red barn caught my eye. A neatly painted sign swung in the breeze: "Frog Pond Farm, Organic Wines." I parked my bike in the driveway and made my way around the barn into the shop.

A nice woman in clean jeans was working behind a wooden counter. There was a pale-blue rag rug on the pine floor and a table with pamphlets and hemp T-shirts sporting the Frog Pond logo for sale. The woman put several wines out on the counter for me to try, and they were delicious.

As we got chatting, I told her I raised organic pork on my farm in North Saanich, and she brought out some wine that went well with pork. It turned out that she had relatives who lived in Sidney. Next she let me try some of their newest wines. It's difficult to grow grapes organically, she said, because some grapes are much less resistant to disease and pests than others. I deduced that was why her bottles of wine were smaller than regular bottles, which I didn't mind at all. I bought a hemp shirt and four bottles of wine and loaded up the basket on the front of my bike. Off I set for home, blissfully happy. I wanted to get there in plenty of time, because our group had tickets to *Major Barbara* that night.

The breeze had turned into a strong wind while I was inside and, as I turned out of the gravel driveway and back onto the main road, I realized that I was rather impaired. It was difficult to steer straight along the edge of the road, especially against the gale. Passing delivery trucks kept honking, and the valuable cargo in the basket kept shifting and sending my bicycle off the edge of the road. Several times I had to make a wobbly halt in the grass, with one hand on the brake and the other on the wine. At one point I mistakenly shifted the bike's gears and found myself pedalling a million miles an hour but going nowhere. Finally my front wheel hit the paved ridge at the side of the road and I wobbled quite without control, in slow motion, into a wet ditch. The wine crashed out of the basket.

Nobody came to my rescue. The wine was okay, though, and I sat in the muddy grass and pulled out my map as if I had intended the whole incident. I had just concluded that I was only a mile or so from town when I saw, in small print at the bottom, "Map Not To Scale." For a moment I worried. Then I realized I didn't really care how far I was from the Pillar and Post: I was very happy, right at that moment, on that muddy slope with my Frog Pond organic wine.

I eventually did make it back to town against the strong wind. As I staggered into the hotel lobby, I noticed it had been autumn-decorated during the day; the place was now full of red and yellow silk mums and stacks of orange gourds in front of the deep chintz couches. I met Maureen in the bar. We had lime daiquiris and I told her all about my adventure.

The two of us walked into town and had burgers at the Angel Inn before seeing *Major Barbara.* After the play we strolled back down Niagara-on-the-Lake's main street. A warm rain was falling, and for some funny reason we found ourselves in the cigar shop I'd seen earlier. We bought two cigars handmade from real leaves in Cuba. Back at the Pillar and Post, we sat outside on a covered patio, under dripping sycamore trees with their grey smooth trunks, to smoke them. Sipping pina coladas, we agreed that the theme of *Major Barbara* corresponded to the slot machine debate going on at home—it was a moral dilemma that pitted one's heart against one's logical mind.

"That's what myths are made of," I said grandly, puffing away.

The next morning our group climbed aboard a new bus headed for Stratford. I dozed off and on in my seat as we drove in a leisurely manner through meadowed countryside dotted with farmhouses, many peaked with lightning rods and weathervanes. A large, flaking billboard proudly read, "Perth County Welcomes You to Canada's Pork Capital."

Stratford appeared without much warning. After we'd checked into our hotel—a plain red box with a dim lobby—Maureen and I decided to walk into town for dinner. It was dark by now and there was a light rain. The main road was noisy, so we cut down onto a side street of big trees and old red-brick houses with verandas. Soon we came upon a pub in what we assumed was the centre of town.

We entered a lobby and took two steps down into a lounge area. It was full of tables of older people eating in absolute silence.

"I'm sorry, we have no room," whispered a thin, aging waitress. "Try next door."

Maureen and I looked at each other. It felt as if we were in a time warp: all those silent people eating mashed potatoes and cutlets. We went next door, to a rather grimy beer parlour, and ordered pork burgers. So far, Stratford was looking rather joyless.

The next morning was grey and overcast. I had a ticket for the matinee of *The Tempest*, and my plan was to wander around town first, then stroll back along the river to the Festival Theatre. It was raining slightly as I set out. I read the brass heritage plaques on various buildings and admired the benches painted a shiny black enamel on almost every corner. When I saw a little sign pointing toward the river that read, "To the Shakespearean Gardens," I turned down a narrow, winding street. The riverbanks were grassy, and there were ducks resting on the shore.

The gardens, which featured herbs and flowers mentioned in Shakespeare's plays, were near a stone bridge, surrounded by a split-rail fence. A small white gazebo with dark-green trim sat at the end of a gravel path. Beyond the gazebo I scaled a chain-link fence and found myself on a small patch of lawn with a nondescript sign reading "Stratford Jail."

Back up on the street, I went into a little shop that had beautiful quilts and raku pottery in the window. Inside, on wooden shelves, bowls and large plates gleamed in gold and almond and green. The quilts, hand sewn in blues and yellows with tiny white stitching, hung on the freshly painted walls. A neatly printed sign said they had been "made by the local Mennonite community." There was some local folk art as well-carved wooden cows and a lovely plump pig. I thought of buying the pig, but I didn't like her mouth. The carver had simply made a slit, yet I know from keeping my sows Mabel and Matilda that pigs can display voluptuous grins of contentment and indulgence.

But then an item on the bottom shelf caught my eye. It was a single tall, glass candlestick that seemed to have a sense of humour. Its base was blue, and orange twists, with yellow beads attached, wound up the stem. Two clear wings with thick white ribs sprouted out halfway up. I decided to buy it. As I was paying, the woman at the counter told me that the candlestick had been there for years, and nobody else had even looked at it. My purchase made me happy. As I walked along the path in the drizzle toward the theatre, I pictured the candlestick in my living room. I thought it would look handsome on the green wooden trunk next to a bouquet of rust-coloured mums and the ceramic green box with funny, curved, gold legs that I bought in Belarus and now keep my matches in.

At the theatre, I found my seat next to an elderly lady wearing headphones to help her hear the play. As I settled in, tucking my candlestick down by my feet, I remembered reading *The Tempest* in a course at the University of Victoria. I'd been moved to tears by Prospero's famous speech about our little lives being rounded with a sleep.

The play opened with William Hutt on a dark stage under a spotlight. He stood tall, dressed in an oatmeal-coloured robe and sandals. He held up a long grey stick to the emotional applause of the crowd, some of whom were already weeping. Then the lights went out, and the action began with a violent shipwreck.

There were some lovely ballet sequences in the play—nymphs with gold-and-blue gossamer wings and exotic, red-and-gold-cloaked characters. William Hutt hobbled about the stage delivering his long speeches with aplomb. Then came the line I was waiting for. He spoke it between clenched teeth, as if cursing creation. Hutt's interpretation was less empathetic than my own, so I felt a little disappointed. I checked my candlestick. It was still there, in its bubble wrap, between my wet running shoes. I wondered why nobody had bought such a unique thing.

The rest of our trip included a visit to Kleinburg to see the McMichael Canadian Art Collection, and a few days in Toronto, where we saw the opera *Macbeth*. Its imaginative set design combined a bloodied plastic curtain, which filled the entire stage, with a soft, emerald-green light, and rows of plastic-covered couches.

Our cultural jaunt ended in Ottawa. We travelled by VIA Rail from Toronto along the lake and through brown meadows dotted with dark groves of evergreens. The scenery reminded me very much of one of Dad's landscape paintings of rural New Brunswick. The leaves of the maples were just beginning to turn a deep, rusty red.

That evening at the National Arts Centre, we went to a concert conducted by Pinchas Zukerman. I loved the music, and I love the name Pinchas. As we boarded the plane for home the next day, I knew it wouldn't be long before Glamorgan Farm had its own inhabitant named Pinchas—my next old SPCA dog, or maybe a new pet pig.

the beauty of disasters

AFTER MY BOOK *Home* came out, I was invited by the B.C. Book Prize organization to go on a reading tour with two children's authors named Marilynn and Earl. We set off from Vancouver one May afternoon in a white van driven by Brian, the tour's cheerful organizer.

After stopping in Hope for a late breakfast, we hit the Coquihalla Highway, headed for Kamloops. The black slate cliffs and fir forest gradually gave way to sagebrush and rolling golden meadows. Along the way, Marilynn, Earl and I had some great chats about what exactly was meant by the term "creative non-fiction." Earl told us he worked for Air Canada, as a security person protecting important travellers. I asked him which famous person in his experience had requested the least protection; he said it was the Dalai Lama. Brian handed us each a bottle of water, and then we travelled in silence for a while.

As Earl fell asleep, and Marilynn closed her eyes, I studied our route on the map in Brian's binder. I felt very contented. It was a perfect moment, and I thought I knew in that instant what the Dalai Lama must know. Then I realized I didn't know anything at all, because I had begun to wish and hope already that this moment would never change.

Mum had told me on the telephone that Kamloops was a wonderful, rustic, cowboy town. It didn't look that way as we drove by strip mall after strip mall filled with tire stores, furniture outlets, fast-food drive-throughs and motels with signs reading "Cheap rooms—outdoor pool." We found our hotel with its towering blue logo just off the main street. The pool was closed for repairs, so I searched out the outdoor hot tub and sat in the chlorinated blue plastic circle in my new turquoise bathing suit, which I had bought a size too small because it was half price. A brown bird with a red plume settled next to the hot tub on the cement. And I thought, "Here I am, alone with a little bird in Kamloops, just the two of us, living out our lives at this hot tub at this moment."

At a small bookstore in downtown Kamloops I bought a copy of Marilynn's book, an illustrated story called *Goodbye to Griffith Street*. It was about a child's experience when his mother packs up and leaves his father. Marilynn describes the Sudbury mining landscape, and the loneliness the boy feels when he tells his friends that he is leaving and they continue playing, as children do. Marilynn had told me the story was based on her own life as a child.

I bought Earl's book, *The Moccasins*, too. It was about his love for his foster mother, her unconditional love for him, and the moccasins she gave him when he was very young that made him feel so safe and cared for.

Marilynn and I walked together to the library for our reading that evening, she in her high heels and me in my running shoes. The librarian was a soft-spoken woman with a blonde bun, silver bracelets and a woven magenta shawl. The three of us read for about 15 people, mostly older women. The idea of the book tour was that we would read to children in the afternoons and to adults in the evening.

The two other stops on our tour were Nanaimo and Port Alberni, both on Vancouver Island. In Nanaimo we were joined in the evening by a writer named Rex, who read from his book about Greenpeace. After the reading in Nanaimo, we all went for a drink in the hotel bar.

The gift shop in the lobby was open late, so before I went up to my room, I bought some gold-plated hummingbird earrings made by a local First Nations artist. The tag in the box explained that the hummingbird represented passion. I couldn't get to sleep that night, because my room was right above the place on the hotel roof where the heating vents blow. I tossed and turned and thought, "If I were the Dalai Lama, how would I deal with this moment?" I thought about my new earrings and wondered if the Dalai Lama ever experienced passion and excitement, or if everything for him was always calm. I began to get drowsy, but before I fell asleep I opened the mini-bar and ate a tube of uniformly sized chips and a pack of cashews, enjoying both immensely.

Port Alberni is nestled in a valley surrounded by scenic mountain ridges. Brian drove us past the K-Mart and the auto junkyard, then down the main street, past the Tim Horton's drive-through and the beer store and the pub on the corner. We parked beside the harbour. Earl struck up a conversation with two First Nations artists who were carving greeting figures with chisels and hatchets; Rex went off to find a drugstore; Brian consulted the map to see where the schools for our readings were, and Marilynn and I strolled along the boardwalk. We all met for lunch at a restaurant called the Clam Bucket.

I ordered a bucket of clams and a carafe of white wine to help prepare me for the tough high-school experience I knew was coming—the last thing big, loping boys with sagging jeans and tattoos wanted was to be read to! I had it in my head that these students would be tough, mill-town kids, quite different from the students I had read to in Kamloops and Nanaimo.

So I had decided to read a story called "The Straw Dolls," about my experience with two little girls in a peasant village in Belarus, where the feast laid on for a Canadian visitor was cubes of pork fat, sour milk, pickled tomatoes, black bread and vodka. I planned to play up the vodka part. Nevertheless, I envied Marilynn and Earl their chance to read to Grade One children. These mill-town boys were going to slaughter me. Down went the carafe of wine with the delicious local clams. Marilynn had a hamburger with fries and a double margarita. I ordered more wine.

Rex knew something of Port Alberni's history, including the tsunami that had caused a big flood in the early 1960s. The conversation went from there to earthquakes, then to lightning storms, plane crashes, hurricanes and forest fires. "Sometimes, disasters are physically beautiful," somebody said. An earthquake might expose layers of rock in sharp shades of mauve and grey; a deadly bomb produces a perfectly symmetrical, orange mushroom cloud over a grey sea; the Challenger space shuttle explodes on take-off in a storm of golden streaks and plumes against a sapphire-blue sky.

Brian paid the bill and we all staggered out to his van. Brian, as the driver, had passed on the alcoholic beverages during lunch. Before we drove off, he handed us each some water. We dropped Marilynn and Earl off at the elementary school, then drove up the hill to the school where Rex and I were reading. Brian let us out at the door, and we walked down the linoleum hall to the office, clutching our water bottles.

A nice man with a whistle around his neck was in the office chatting to the secretary. "Oh, yes," he smiled. "The kids are looking forward to your readings."

Like hell, I thought, feeling a bit sick.

"You'll be reading to Mr. Morrison's history class," he said to Rex, and then to me, "Anny, you'll be reading to Mrs. Chandler's drama class."

Rex and I looked at each other in shock. The teachers must have actually read our books and placed us with appropriate students. I'd been in the school for 10 minutes, and so far I hadn't witnessed anyone being mugged or heard an obscene word echoing down the hallway. In fact, a group of excited girls were in the hall with a teacher, patting a stray kitten they had found.

The young drama teacher met me at the door of her classroom. The students were smiling and lounging on the carpeted floor in front of my chair, which had a bottle of water on it. A blond boy was resting his head on another boy's leg. The students listened as their teacher suggested that perhaps this author (me) would give everyone some insights into the human condition, because that's what she (the teacher) thought my book was about. The students clapped and I thanked them for inviting me.

First I told them about my two trips to Belarus: the Minsk orphanage; the KGB building; my second trip, when I was locked up for bringing cargo to the orphans. I told them about Chernobyl and the nuclear contamination there, and I described the peasant villages I had visited where at least one person in every family had thyroid cancer. I showed them some photographs I had taken and the blue-glass vodka bottles I had brought home as a souvenir of the time I'd been held by the KGB. Then I read "The Straw Dolls."

When I had finished, the class sat up and clapped. Many hands went up together when I asked if there were any questions. They were mostly curious about my second visit, when I'd been detained and interrogated. Then, thank goodness, somebody asked, "Do they have movies and videos in Belarus?" and things lightened up for a moment.

A dark-haired girl came up and asked if I would sign her copy of my book, which I did. Then she said, "I am a Romanian orphan and I have a photograph book of my family and my village. The authorities gave it to me when I left." The class remained silent as I asked her what she remembered of the country and the orphanage. And then I had a flash of amazement that here we all were, in a classroom in Port Alberni.

Brian drove us back to Nanaimo late that night, making sure we had lots of water to drink along the way. I lay awake in my hotel bed for a long time, both stimulated and sad. I remembered Mum telling me about a day she'd been painting at her easel. She was frustrated, and she sat looking at the canvas for a long time. And then, she said, out of nowhere, "Something floated by and I caught it." It was the same thing as connecting with the students in that class. You never know what lies ahead in the next moment, or what might come floating by.

I was up very early the next morning and Marilynn was too. We bumped into one another on the street. We walked down onto some wooden docks bobbing in the water and found a blue-and-white café at the end of the wharf, where we sat outside and had coffee and buns full of bacon and eggs and cheese.

Marilynn pulled a small paper bag out of her purse. "I bought this for you in Kamloops," she said. Inside the bag was a card with a beautiful picture of the Dalai Lama. He was standing somewhere, looking dark brown and tanned, with red and yellow swaths of cloth draped around his shoulders. He was smiling.

flying alone

I WAS A NERVOUS LITTLE girl, rather high-strung, and I worried all the time. The place I felt the calmest was with my Gran at her home on Galiano Island. To my immense pleasure, I often spent summers there with her and her husband, Jack. I called him Uncle Jack, or "Unk."

Galiano was a quiet, peaceful place. In the warm, dry meadows, the grasses and wildflowers came up to my waist. Small, painted shake-and-shingle houses dotted the landscape. The lanes were lined with blackberry hedgerows, and there was always a smell of wild roses and dry fir trees. Smooth, rounded sandstone caves and interesting rock structures formed much of the waterfront.

Uncle Jack was an old fisherman, and his hands were covered in flaking callouses. Each callous represented a jab from a different fish hook, he claimed, and he told me about each adventure. We'd sit in Gran's kitchen, at the table with the blue-and-white checkered cloth and the chipped yellow pot full of sweet peas. Uncle Jack would take a wooden match and gently clean the outer rim of his right ear with it before lighting his pipe. He sat stooped over in his green overalls, his ruddy face with its protruding lower lip serious as he began to tell each tale. He'd glance up from time to time, then grin a little as he came to each story's happy ending. Once when my favourite troll, Isabelle, had a toothache, Uncle Jack led us to his workshop in the woodshed out under the plum tree. We put Isabelle under a blanket, and Unk pulled her tooth with his pliers while I held her down.

Gran, my mother's mum, was a strong, independent woman. She had built a huge rock garden, and I'd often see her standing in it with a hose, watering the Canterbury bells and larkspur, her bare legs all scratched up and bitten by insects. A neighbour's bull once charged down her driveway headed for her garden, but Gran grabbed the rake and yelled, and the bull took off through the grassy meadow instead.

At night, Gran would read to me from *Grimm's Fairy Tales* as I lay in my little cot with its cool white sheets in her front room. The bedroom always smelled of Raid, which I loved. Gran wore blue cotton smocks from Sears, and when she gardened she always put her false teeth in one of the pockets. Then she'd forget and wash the smock, sending her teeth through the wringer. There was always clean white laundry on the line in the yard, and I was fascinated with Gran's underwear—her underpants were so large!

I had a small tent made from blankets set up in the garden. My trolls lived there—I had more than 30 of them. The tent was also where I stashed treasures such as seashells from Montague Beach. Montague Beach was a miracle of nature, covered in pure-white crushed clamshell, with hard black lava formations jutting out into the bottle-green water. We often went there in Uncle Jack's rusted old blue Austin. Gran and Unk would sit on a log and talk while I puttered around in the warm, shallow water for hours. The shore was lined with windswept yew trees and arbutus, its paper-thin red bark peeling off the elegant trunks.

Wild cats were everywhere on Galiano, and one summer I befriended a mangy tabby I named Gracie. Gracie would visit my backyard tent, and Gran would let me feed her and give her a dish of milk. Sometimes the little cat would leave a mouse on my pillow there. It was an idyllic life. When I got tired of playing with my trolls or organizing my seashells, I'd write stories and illustrate them with coloured markers.

Sometimes Gran and Uncle Jack drove down to Bambrick's village store near the ferry for supplies. Old Mr. Bambrick used to let me eat dog biscuits from the bins in the back, and I'd crouch on the floor chewing the orange, dog-boned-shaped cookies while Gran shopped and posted her letters. Afterwards we would visit Gran's friend Flo Bellhouse, who had a small white cottage on Sturdies Bay, where the ferry docked at the end of the creosoted, planked wharf. Another of Gran's friends, Stanley Page, drove the island taxi and lived on a grand old farm full of apple trees. Galiano's postman, Donald New, was a tanned, bald man. Everyone always said how remarkable it was that he could walk around barefoot, even in the blackberries, and never feel a thing. Years later, Mum told me that Donald was a nudist. I hadn't even noticed, being totally fixated on his tough feet.

Sadly, the summers always had to end. Usually Mum flew out to get me, but one year, when I was six, she couldn't, so my godmother Barbara (Mum's best friend from childhood), who lived in West Vancouver, came over to Galiano to pick me up. The plan was that I'd fly back east alone and Mum would meet me in Toronto. She and Dad had spent the summer in Spain, painting. She still has the thick green vermouth glasses they bought there on some island.

I loved Barbara's home on Roseberry Avenue. It was calm and cool and quiet, and it smelled of cedar. You walked in from the shaded driveway, and the living room was large, with lots of windows. There was a view of the sea, and of Vancouver. The little red dots you could see were the tankers anchored in the harbour. Barbara's living room had a great stone fireplace and rattan furniture; the base of the lamp in the corner was an enormous amber bottle.

Barbara had a daughter, Lesley, who was a little older than me. I shared Les's bedroom and was in awe of her treasures. She had a collection of exotic tropical corals and shells from Hawaii with pink shiny interiors on her dresser, along with a blue shell bracelet and delicate glass vials of white sand. One day when Les was out, I had a picnic on the front lawn under the monkey puzzle tree, with all of her teddy bears and my trolls.

On the day I was to fly home, I wore a brown dress with black diamonds on it and a pair of leotards. Barbara and Les drove me to the airport and walked with me across the tarmac to the plane. At the bottom of the tall aluminum steps, Barbara gave me a brown paper shopping bag. It was full of presents, brightly wrapped in colourful tissue paper, and she said that I was to open all of them during my trip.

A stewardess led me up the stairs and buckled me into my seat, placing the shopping bag at my feet. I watched Barbara and Les go back into the terminal through my hazy, grey, oval window. After a few minutes, a thin woman with her hair in a bun sat down next to me. She was wearing a short, bright-yellow paper dress (paper dresses were all the rage at the time), and I could see her tanned, sinewy thighs on the seat.

I began to feel sick. I felt sicker and sicker but didn't want to tell anyone. (I'm still like that!) When the stewardess brought the thin lady a newspaper, I finally said to her in a nervous little voice, "I think I'm going to be sick," and she snapped back, "You can't be sick, there's no turbulence." (Which I thought was an odd thing to say, since we hadn't left the tarmac.) Just as she was saying, "There's an air-sick bag in front of your seat," I threw up into her lap. I could see her yellow dress absorbing the liquid, and then the paper gently pulled apart.

Once we were airborne, I opened a present wrapped in blue tissue. It was a pack of crayons, and Les had added some of her lovely pink and white Hawaiian shells.

h e y , m a !

THE SUMMER I WAS SEVEN, I went to stay with my Polish grandparents in Toronto. Babi (which means "old woman") and Dziadzik
(which means "old man") lived on Ossington Avenue, a busy street
full of traffic, in a small, green, asphalt-shingled house with red trim
and a peaked roof. Their house smelled of old carpet and boiling cabbage and potatoes. At the end of a narrow dark hall hung a picture of
Jesus. As Dziadzik had once pointed out to me, Jesus's eyes seemed to
follow you around.

As Mum unpacked my bag in a small bedroom with slanted
ceilings, I started to get an empty, lonely feeling. Babi was making
cabbage rolls downstairs and Dziadzik was yelling about something.
He was always yelling, in a sort of panic. "Hey, Ma," he'd scream, as
if he had just broken his leg, and then he would yell something in
Polish. Babi would just sigh and keep stirring whatever was in the big
aluminum pot on the stove.

Off the kitchen was a room with lots of windows. On one wall there were several shelves of dolls dressed in colourful Polish costumes. On another set of shelves were Dziadzik's cactus plants, in little clay pots that he had painted different colours. He was always decorating things—he couldn't help it. Above the door to the backyard he had hung a hand-painted sign that read, "Wont yu come into my Garden?"

When I woke up the next morning, I could hear Dziadzik yelling in Polish. He was a big, rough, dark man with a mouth full of bad teeth. I went downstairs, rather nervously, and Dziadzik was standing there under his garden sign holding a huge glass mug of coffee. He yelled at me, "Hey, grandchild!" And then he yelled at Babi, "Hey, Ma—give the grandchild coffee," and then back at me, "Hey, hey, put milk, put sugar!" He was frantic and loud, but I didn't really mind—I liked the attention. Dziadzik and I took our coffee out to the yard and sat on the plastic chairs beside the cabbage patch as the sun rose over the sooty brick industrial buildings across the alley. He slurped and gulped and burped, and I followed suit.

After that, I drank a mug of coffee every morning in the garden with Dziadzik. When our coffee was finished we would water the garden. He gave me a little watering can with my name painted on it and yelled, "Hey, hey, water this, and water that."

Soon, I didn't miss Mum or Dad at all—I became Dziadzik's sidekick. He took me to his Polish clubs in rundown community centres, to bars and poker halls, and I met his bedraggled, grey-haired friends.

I felt like one of the boys. Babi stayed home to cook and do laundry, which she hung up on a string in the backyard. Dziadzik's baggy white underpants with their faint brown stains swung gently above the cabbages.

One time, after we'd drunk our coffee and watered the cabbage plants, Dziadzik took me to a funeral home, where I saw a dead woman in a coffin. She had on a black dress with a white lace collar, and there were bouquets of roses on a counter. Dziadzik just looked in the coffin and gave a grunt.

On our way home we went to a lumberyard, where Dziadzik bought some long two-by-fours. He yelled at me to put one end on my shoulder, and he carried the other. We stood waiting for a bus, but when it came, Dziadzik and the bus driver had a yelling match about taking the wood on board. Dziadzik won, but we couldn't get it on the bus anyway. So we walked back across Toronto, through the heat and the smog and the grit and the traffic. I went first, with the boards on my shoulder and Dziadzik shouting directions at me from behind. I enjoyed the jaunt. When we got home, Babi served us soup with plums.

Some afternoons Babi and I would sit on the red sofa in the dark front room and go through frayed black photo albums. I wasn't as interested in the photos as I was in Babi's lilting voice, which gave me tingles up the back of my head and sent me off into a kind of trance. The photos were of peasant women in smock dresses and aprons digging and hauling cabbages and potatoes in muddy fields.

As Babi rambled on, "Ah, mama with sister…," I would drift into a blissful dream of one day growing cabbages of my own.

On the morning that Mum was to pick me up, Babi scrubbed me from head to toe after I'd had my coffee with Dziadzik. I put on some yellow shorts and a white blouse and went to play in the dusty park down the street. When I got back, Dziadzik began to shout, "Hey, Ma! Hey, Ma! She all dirty!" But when Mum arrived all she said was, "Oh, Anny looks like she's been well fed." I had grown that summer, and developed some solid peasant muscles too.

all you can eat

DAD HAD A BROTHER NAMED Ernie, whom he had not seen for years. All we knew was that Ernie lived alone in St. Catharines, Ontario, and was a pantyhose salesman. Mum resumed contact with Ernie the summer I was turning 13, when she received a letter from his son, and she and I flew out to visit him.

We took a bus from the Toronto airport to St. Catharines and waited at the station until Ernie pulled up in a dented grey delivery van. Ernie was much bigger and taller than Dad, bald, with a kind face and a gold tooth. He wore glasses and a rust-coloured cardigan over a white shirt and grey pants. He was a real gentleman, taking our bags and opening the van door for Mum. We loved him right away.

We drove through congested traffic, then pulled into a driveway off a busy road. Ernie's house was a box painted bright green, with a small patch of lawn in front. Inside, everything was beige and spotless. In one half of the living room was a bar that Ernie had built himself, with black vinyl bar stools. Ernie took our bags down the hall to a bedroom with two single beds in a maple bedroom suite. The bedroom window looked out at an equally neat grey stucco house next door.

Ernie made Mum a cup of tea, then got himself a bottle of beer and a tall glass mug. He put out a bowl of Cheezies and chips and a can of mixed nuts, all of which he retrieved from a shelf behind the bar. We sat in his living room and chatted. There was a white lacy curtain over the front window, and I could see the traffic going by outside.

Later, we sat out on the cement patio. Ernie barbecued some hamburgers and put out an array of red and yellow condiments in plastic squirt containers. Mum and I had made a salad with an iceberg lettuce and a bottle of Kraft blue-cheese dressing. After the sun went down, Mum and I turned in, but Ernie stayed up and watched sports on his big TV set.

The next day, Ernie offered to take me on his rounds while Mum went to Hamilton to visit Dad and Ernie's parents—they had moved from Toronto. We drove all over St. Catharines delivering beige pantyhose in purple cellophane packages to stores. We stopped at a Polish café in a hot, gritty suburb for lunch, and Ernie ordered us an enormous plate of perogies. Some were filled with plums, and some with cheese. I had an orange float to top it all off. My uncle and I had discovered we had something in common—voracious appetites. The sun beat down as we stopped in at more strip malls and stores in suburbs with our deliveries. We took a break in mid-afternoon at the Dairy Queen, where we ordered banana splits.

When Mum and I were lying in our single beds that night, I asked her if Uncle Ernie could come and stay with us in Fredericton. She said she would arrange it.

Late one rainy night that autumn, Mum and Dad and I drove out to the Fredericton airport to meet him. Dad had a funny smirk on his face as he ambled over to the arrival area. I was so excited—I could see the plane's lights heading right toward us on the wet black tarmac.

Gradually, people with shoulder bags began to drift into the terminal. Then we saw Ernie, lumbering toward the glass doors carrying a brown paper shopping bag and a duffle bag. He and Dad embraced. Ernie was twice the size of Dad, and moved half as fast.

Because Ernie was so tall, he sat in the front seat of our green Buick with Dad for the drive home. At one point he spotted the Ponderosa Steakhouse. "Oh," he said with delight as he turned to me, "we'll make a trip there!" When we got to the house Ernie pulled out all sorts of things from his brown shopping bag: a long string of Polish garlic sausages, a huge loaf of black bread and a case of Polish beer.

Dad took us out on a lake in his aluminum boat the next day. He had loaded the car with fishing rods, and Mum had packed a picnic. While Dad and Ernie fished off in the warm brown water, Mum sketched wildflowers and I played on the pebble beach with my trolls.

We headed home late in the afternoon with Dad and Ernie's lake bass in a white plastic bucket. They filleted the fish out on the back porch while Mum made apple jelly with some wild apples she and I had picked in an abandoned orchard. Dad and Ernie had a drink in

Dad's garden, and then we all sat down at our wooden picnic table and ate Polish sausage and sardines on thin squares of black bread sprinkled with fresh dill. Later, when we got hungry again, Ernie took me out alone to the Ponderosa for a pizza.

Ernie stayed with us for a week, and at about the middle point of his visit he met a big, happy, red-headed woman named Ethel. Ethel was a real estate agent who loved fishing—she knew every good fishing hole in rural New Brunswick. She came by for Ernie in a red station wagon with wood panelling on the side, and two huge pairs of green rubber hip waders in the back. Ernie went off with her for the afternoon carrying the brand-new fishing tackle box he'd bought at Canadian Tire. Ethel honked as they pulled out of our driveway.

Ethel came for supper one night after Ernie had gone back to Ontario. I was upstairs when I heard her say in a gay tone, "Oh, Bruno, I loved your brother Ernie. Isn't it a shame that he's paralyzed from the waist down."

After that first visit, Ernie came to see us every couple of months. Then, one time, he brought with him a woman named Elma. They had met at Arthur Murray's Ballroom Dance Studio. Elma was a buxom, buck-toothed, retired schoolteacher who wore mauve polyester pantsuits, and knitted turquoise toilet-paper and Kleenex-box covers in her spare time. She played bridge with "the girls" and knew all the places to eat brunch for $2.95 in the St. Catharines area. Ernie told Mum that Elma was a "real lady" and quite a catch.

Mum and Dad and I were invited to the wedding, which was held at the St. Catharines Polish Hall. Mum made me wear a dress we'd bought at Zellers in Fredericton. The hall was packed with our Polish relatives, who danced a ferocious polka around the newlyweds.

We rarely saw Ernie after he married Elma. At some point they moved to Rice Lake, Ontario. Mum visited them there once, and she told us that Elma had placed teddy bears made of pink fluff on all the beds. My eating days with Uncle Ernie had ended. But whenever I ordered a pizza at the Ponderosa Steakhouse, I always thought of him.

h e n r y

DAD AND ERNIE HAD ANOTHER brother, Henry, but neither of
them had seen him since childhood. Dad and Ernie and Henry, as
very small boys, had emigrated with Dziadzik and their mother from
Poland, with absolutely nothing to their name. The family lived under
a bridge in Toronto and ate restaurant cabbage scraps. After a short
time, their mother left them, out of despair, and the story is that she
died a young, sad death. The last time Dad saw her was in a school-
yard when he was in kindergarten; his mother was standing on the
other side of the chain-link fence.

Later on Dziadzik married Babi, and she raised the boys. When
they grew up, Ernie and Dad stayed in touch with Dziadzik and Babi,
but Henry, who was older, left town and was never seen or heard from
again—until Ernie spotted his name in a Buffalo newspaper, right
around the time he began to visit us in Fredericton. The article was
by a born-again Christian woman from Louisiana, and it was about an

old man who lived on a boat on a canal. People called him Santa Claus, because he made wooden toys for the local church to give to poor children. The man's name was Henry Bobak. Ernie contacted Henry and drove down to Baton Rouge with Elma to visit him.

A year later, Mum and Dad made the trip. As Mum tells it, the visit was an absolute disaster. It was a hazy, muggy day when Mum and Dad arrived at the canal. They located the chief caretaker of the wharf, a fat, angry-looking young man in long baggy shorts, and asked him where they might find Henry. The caretaker carried two guns in holsters, one on each hip. The wharf was lined with rundown boats sitting in the canal's gasoline sludge.

Mum says that Dad wanted to turn around and leave as they walked down the rickety wharf in the 90-degree heat. Henry was sitting on a plastic lawn chair beside his rusted little boat, which was called *The Gypsy*. He had a thick white beard stained yellow by cigarette smoke.

Henry had filled his ancient fridge with food for his new-found family, and he'd arranged for Mum and Dad to sleep on an empty boat down the wharf. The Christian lady showed up, and that night the four of them went to a local restaurant and ate shrimp cocktails. Henry called Mum "Sis."

The next morning, at the crack of dawn, Dad told Mum they were leaving, and they did.

The born-again lady wrote to Mum a year later. She sent a Hallmark card emblazoned with a cream-coloured bouquet of roses, announcing that Henry Bobak had passed away.

on the road with frankenstein

i: the zipper

WHEN I WAS 14, MUM took me to a play called *The Playboy of the Western World*. It was at The Playhouse, Fredericton's professional theatre. There was lots of money put toward the arts in Canada in those days, and The Playhouse was magnificent, a big, white-brick building surrounded by elm trees with a granite patio in front. It sat next door to the copper-domed legislative building, and across the street from the elegant Beaverbrook Art Gallery. On The Playhouse roof was a white box that looked like a big package with strips of blue, red and yellow ribbon wrapped around it every which way. This box was the "fly gallery," I would later learn, the area inside the theatre used for raising and lowering sets for different scenes on pulleys.

The director of *The Playboy of the Western World* was Bill Glassco, a friend of Mum's from Toronto. I didn't really understand the play, but I was enthralled with the experience of going to the theatre. Bill invited us backstage after the show, and I was in awe. There was a captivating, intoxicating energy to the place, an unreal feeling that totally drew me in.

My life at the time consisted of attending junior high at Albert Street School and riding my horse, Missy, who was stabled at the local racetrack, Wilmot Downs. Albert Street School was a large, light-green, stucco box full of sexy girls and a little grey principal who wore clip-on ties and lectured us on "future goals." Every day after school I escaped on my bike to go take care of Missy, a Palomino Mum had bought me from a farmer up the Nashwalk River. Missy was getting old, though, and much as I loved the rustic, easy life of the racetrack, I was feeling a bit restless. Lots of girls my age had begun to acquire boyfriends; they'd hang out at fast-food places or go to junior high school dances or go shopping. I found a farm in a nearby village that would take Missy, and I decided to join the theatre.

Mum knew the artistic director at The Playhouse, and she asked him if he would see me one day after school. I rode my bike down to the theatre for an interview. I was wearing a red ski jacket and green corduroy pants, and I was a little down because I had just failed a math test.

The director was nice—a large man with big lips. He asked me what I would like to do, and I said, "Anything you need." We talked for a while, and then the director said he'd allow me to come every day after school and help out backstage. I was thrilled.

My first job at The Playhouse was in the props area. The next production coming up was the farce *A Flea in Her Ear.* The set was all pink and silver, quite elaborate, with twirling velvet sofas and hanging lamps. The action in the play was loud and funny, full of misunderstandings, and it took place in a hotel. I helped make a curtain by crunching up hundreds of tinfoil balls and stringing them together. It was dull, though, as I sat there at a high black counter doing my little task. Nobody paid much attention to me.

Upstairs in the wardrobe department they were sewing flapper-type dresses for the leading actresses, and one afternoon I heard a big row. One of the actresses, a plump Irish woman, stormed out of the fitting room yelling, "You need to go back to seamstress school!" She marched down the stairs half-naked in a pair of high heels, her big white belly flopping up and down. Her broad rear end looked quite strange under her beige pantyhose. As she was storming into her dressing room, she saw me standing aghast in the dim hallway. "Bring me the director," she snapped. "I need to tell him I cannot work with that cow of a wardrobe mistress." Then she slammed her dressing-room door.

I went to tell the director, a pale, tired-looking man with a ponytail, that the actress wanted to see him. As I went back to crumpling up my silver balls, I could hear her shouting at him, "She said I was fat! She said that I have put on weight since she first took the measurements! She couldn't even get my zipper done up, for Christ's sakes! I don't need this type of treatment! She's a goddamn hag!" Then she began to cry.

I knew the actress was from Toronto, and I suddenly recognized her shrill voice—she was the lady who did the air-freshener commercial! I was star-struck. The ad appeared regularly during the family-court TV program I was addicted to. When the director had finished talking to the actress, he asked if I would go upstairs to fetch the wardrobe mistress.

It was all very glamorous, and I felt so important delivering the message. The wardrobe mistress was a dowdy woman in a baggy grey dress. She had a cigarette dangling from her lip, and a bunch of pins were stuffed in there as well, and was hemming a red satin dress on a dressmaker's dummy. The wardrobe room was a mess of luxurious fabrics on big wooden tables, with drawings and patterns pinned to every wall.

After I had made my request, the wardrobe mistress spat out the pins, removed her cigarette and said, "Give the old bag this message." She scrawled something on a piece of paper in big black letters and handed it to me. I read it on the way back down the stairs. "You Can't Make a Silk Purse Out Of a Sow's Ear," it said.

I knocked on the actress's dressing-room door. "Come in," she called, sounding calmer. She seemed to be over her anger now, and she was lounging in her chair dressed in a lavender silk bathrobe. She was smoking French cigarettes from a blue cellophane package and drinking Scotch—I could see the bottle on the counter amidst pots and jars and sticks of makeup. Something intuitive told me not to give her the wardrobe mistress's message. Seeing the actress's rage and her big flopping stomach and wide behind had made me feel sorry for her. I didn't really know what to say, so I blurted out, "I'm sure they can get the zipper to fit."

"Thank you, dahhling," the actress replied in her lovely soft Irish accent. "Would you like a cigarette? A drink?" I declined, although I was no stranger to whisky from my racetrack days. I had watched plenty of old grooms drink it and pass out in the hay.

Bright light bulbs were blazing around the dressing-room mirror, and the heat accentuated the smell of greasepaint and worn powder puffs. The actress was dabbing her neck with some kind of vanilla musk. I stood there for a few more moments completely speechless, almost in love, definitely in awe. I wanted to take care of her, this big famous Toronto actress who did air-freshener commercials.

My next job in the prop shop was to sort out a bucketful of screws and nails. I sat at my counter for hours on end while long-haired, bearded men in jeans put the huge sets together around me. Opening night was a week away. I had begun to pick bouquets of wild daisies, Indian paintbrush and buttercups from the nearby riverbank for the actress, and I'd leave them on her dressing table every afternoon while she was rehearsing. Every day she left me a little note thanking me. I progressed to cleaning her ashtray, washing her whisky glass and hanging up her bathrobe before going back to my menial sorting job.

The director of the play approached me on a day when I was feeling particularly bored with the nails. "I would like you to be the lead actress's dresser," he said. "Please start coming to rehearsals so you can learn where her changes are." It was the happiest day of my life. I would make *sure* her zipper did up!

The next time I knocked on the actress's door, I felt very qualified to ask, "Is there anything I can do for you?" And from then on, I spent my time at The Playhouse catering to her every need. I memorized her lines and her costume changes, and I did manage to get her zipper done up, by gently saying to her, "Just suck in a little—there we go—you look perfect." I combed her wig, bought her cigarettes and organized her costumes; I helped her dress and undress and made sure she had clean towels in her shower. I even cleaned her soap dish, and I still brought her bouquets of flowers.

When school let out for the summer, I began to spend every waking hour at The Playhouse. I was soon promoted to taking care of all of the actors and their costumes, although I remained most loyal to my first love. There was a lovely, rather feminine actor who played support roles. He asked for nothing, but we had long chats. In between scenes he read poetry. I took him flowers, too, and I worked extra hard on cleaning his white shirts.

Once a week I rode my moped, which had replaced my old bike, out to the country to visit Missy. She was usually standing in the meadow, enjoying her retirement. I groomed her and washed her and put fly spray on her, cleaned her hooves and gave her apples, but my heart was now in the theatre.

ii: frankenstein on tour

In September of that year, I started high school. At noon, all the kids hung out at Tim Horton's or smoked in the parking lot of Canadian Tire across the street. I was failing math and not interested in dating. But I had got my driver's licence, after three tries, and I was regularly drinking Singapore Slings with the actors at The Playhouse.

In late autumn, The Playhouse put on a play called *Frankenstein*, adapted from Mary Shelley's novel by the Fredericton poet Alden Nowlan and the director of The Playhouse, Walter Learning. I was swept away with emotion at the sad, sad plight of the monster who wanted to die from loneliness—he had never asked to be created, but there he was, alive and huge and ugly in our world. In the dark wings, as I helped the actors change from black capes to white coats, I would weep.

In the play, Baron von Frankenstein had two bumbling servants who provided comic relief and assisted in the set changes. They were buffoons, characters who would occasionally have their ears boxed for being incompetent. One of those servants was played by a tough little actor named Johnny. He was small and stooped, but he had a twinkle in his eye and a sly sense of humour. He wore a blue bead on a leather strap around his weathered neck.

Johnny and I became friends. He drank so much rum before each performance that I had to push him on stage saying "Trunk scene!" or "Garden scene!" He'd fumble around out there, to lots of laughter, completely impaired. It was no act. In his dressing room after the show, I'd help him change out of his servant costume—red velvet pants tucked into black leather boots and a baggy white shirt—and then walk him back to his hotel next to the Metropolitan Store on Queen Street.

When I heard that *Frankenstein* was going to tour the Atlantic provinces, my heart leapt. I had to go along, I just *had* to. I didn't care about school—I could miss a month and make up math later. I was sure I could persuade Mum to let me go.

One night after the show I asked the director of The Playhouse about it. I could be so useful on tour, I explained as convincingly as I could. I knew every wig and every costume and every actor's habit. The director wouldn't say yes or no just then, and as the weeks passed I almost lost my mind with anxiety. I cried and cussed and pleaded and begged, and still he wouldn't tell me. Red-faced and exhausted, but determined nonetheless, I asked again a few days before the show was set to leave. "I'll think about it," the director said. But I had had all I could take. I locked myself in Johnny's dressing room with all the costumes and refused to come out until the director gave me an answer.

The audience was seated, the show was about to begin and nobody had their costumes on. Finally the director called through the door, said, "Okay, you can tour, but under my conditions, which I will tell you tomorrow."

I opened the door. Johnny was standing there in his white underpants, holding a rum bottle. "You tell them, sweetheart," he said. I couldn't have been more elated.

iii: the blue bead

The next day when I arrived at the theatre, I was called into the director's office. "These are your conditions for going on the tour," he told me. "Your job will be to do the laundry every day for the actors. You will drive on ahead of the trucks to set up their dressing rooms, and you must share a room with Johnny, because nobody else will." I can't remember now if I told Mum and Dad about that last condition or not.

There was a Canadian film out at the time that everyone was talking about, called *Goin' down the Road*, and Mum took me to see it at the university one night before I left on tour. The movie is about two unemployed men from rural Nova Scotia with big dreams of finding work in Toronto. They are broke, and they sleep with any woman who will take them. They drink too much and talk big and their car breaks down on Yonge Street, in front of a famous record store. I loved the film. I recognized the sadness of their dreams of life in the big city. They were such hopeful losers, destined to blow every opportunity, and one of them in particular never lost his sense of humour or optimism. Above all, I was amazed to find that one of the men was played by my friend Johnny!

The crew at The Playhouse loaded up several big trucks with the collapsible set for *Frankenstein*. White vans with black letters spelling out "Frankenstein on Tour" would transport the actors. The van I was to drive carried the wigs and costumes and the actors' belongings. As part of the crew, I'd be driving a day ahead of the actors to set up the show.

On a crisp, sunny morning, our posse of vans and trucks pulled out of The Playhouse's parking lot and headed north to Edmonston, New Brunswick, along the Trans-Canada Highway. The road followed the Saint John River, which was framed on either side by rolling green meadows and forests of burnt orange, reds and yellows. Small white wooden houses dotted the riverbank.

We pulled into Edmonston late in the afternoon and checked into a motel. Most of the crew headed to the local high school auditorium to assemble the set. I drove down the main street looking for a laundromat, and a hairdresser who could prepare the leading lady's wig. Many of the shop signs were in French, I noticed. The street was grimy, lined with little brown stucco shops. There was a laundromat next to the beer parlour, so I pulled in. I scrubbed the white collars on the costumes with a small brush and some Wisk the wardrobe mistress had given me, then loaded everything into mustard-coloured washers.

The beauty salon a few shops down was closed for the day, but I figured I could fix the wig later myself. I had a few walnut crunchies at the Tim Horton's down the street while I waited for the costumes and towels to dry. The walnut crunchy wasn't a real doughnut, but more like a big square of glazed chocolate cake. I could eat about 10 of them at one sitting.

The crew and I met up at the motel for supper, and then we went back to the school. I organized the two dressing rooms, hanging the clean costumes on metal hangers and setting out each actors' section by placing their makeup kits in front of the small, round, portable mirrors on the room's arborite counters. I placed a clean glass for water beside each makeup box and a small ashtray. Every actor smoked, and every actor except Johnny carried a package of breath mints. I fluffed up the red wig, then put it back on its Styrofoam head, placing it at the leading actress's spot.

It was 1:00 AM when we returned to the motel. This was better than math homework any day! My room had an orange shag carpet and two beds covered in floral polyester bedspreads. The bathroom was olive green, with a stained shower curtain and a rubber bath mat with black mould on the sucker things underneath. I went to sleep blissfully happy.

The next morning I was up before any of the crew. There was a little frost outside on the black asphalt, and a yellow strip of sunrise was visible above the grey hills. I had a huge breakfast at the motel diner, ordering "Hot cakes with fruit topping" (pancakes smothered in canned cherries and piles of whipped cream from a squirt can) and sausages. The actors arrived that afternoon. The Edmonston audience loved *Frankenstein*, and they clapped enthusiastically from their grey plastic chairs, set up in rows in the gymnasium.

I felt the monster's pain, and his relief at dying, night after night after night as I drove the costume van from one small town to the next throughout New Brunswick, Nova Scotia and Prince Edward Island. By the time we reached PEI, the red-clay potato fields were asleep under three feet of snow. All the gymnasiums were alike, with floppy cloth team banners pinned on their plywood walls: the Bathurst Bears, the Woodstock Wolverines, the Saint John Sabres, the Halifax Hornets.

After the show, late at night, Johnny and I would sit on our beds, leaning against the arborite headboards. He would drink his whisky and I would eat doughnuts. The next morning I would get up at dawn and start the van, which was full of damp costumes stained with makeup from the evening before. The parking lots were covered with black ice, and the tailpipe exhaust showed white in the sharp air. I'd leave Johnny fast asleep in the dark room with his blue duffle bag and his worn black leather boots at the foot of his bed.

It was a stormy day when we made the crossing to Newfoundland. White-capped grey waves slapped the sides of the ferry as we sat upstairs on vinyl benches in the lounge. In the days that followed, we visited Stephenville, Corner Brook and other little towns along the road to St. John's. I fell in love with the province. It was a rugged place, but it seemed gentle; there was a special type of ease in the dramatic landscape. Later, I'd have the same feeling about certain parts of Russia—the landscape embodied calm, but with an underlying drama.

The show's final performance was in St. John's, and I felt a deep melancholy sinking into me that night. After the show, Johnny and I were sitting as usual in our room, this time in a rundown Holiday Inn on the main street. He was flying to Toronto the next morning, and the crew and I were scheduled to start driving the grimy vans and trucks back to Fredericton at the crack of dawn. I was thinking that my life was about to end. In a week, I'd be back in the monstrous yellow-brick high school next to the strip mall on a bleak, icy hill in Fredericton.

I was sitting dejectedly on the edge of my bed when Johnny put down his whisky bottle. He pulled the leather strap with the blue bead on it over his head and handed it to me. "Wear this and then pass it on," he said in his husky voice, "to someone who needs it after you." And then he went to sleep, with his boots still on.

The next morning I drove out of the Holiday Inn parking lot at a freezing 4:00 AM, wearing my blue bead. The tour was over and, although I didn't know it, I would never see or hear of Johnny again.

I stopped at the Stephenville car wash to clean the grit, sand and salt off the van, and it was gleaming white again as I set off along a winding road lined with jagged brown rocks. In the cold light of early morning, I drove toward the ferry that would take me back across the tossing, steel-grey sea.

stan

THE AFTERNOON AFTER MY FINAL day of high school, I boarded a train from Fredericton Junction to Vancouver. I had one large suitcase full of clothes, my 36 trolls and a braided piece of blonde hair from my old horse, Missy. I was leaving home, going out west where I felt I belonged.

High school had been a trial, and I'd graduated with a C- average. My worst subject was math, and to this day numbers make my stomach turn. I had a vague interest in history, and the term we studied France I did some research and wrote that the members of the court of Louis XVI didn't bathe because of inadequate plumbing, but instead used copious amounts of perfume. Our teacher was a small, wiry man who wore suits and clip-on ties and dark-rimmed glasses. He gave me a C- on my essay. On the page where I explained about the perfume, he had written, "You've got to be kidding!?!?"

My best subject was gym, where I excelled in running due to

sheer will and loneliness, passing the plump, soft girls who'd stopped in a bushy corner for a smoke and a discussion of their recent exploits with boys. The gym teacher was patient and calm as he taught me how to swim, and I remember thinking I could tread water forever as he graded me on his clipboard. He gave me a little confidence in those years, although later I heard he was fired for flirting with a sexy blonde student.

Mum and Dad had driven me to the station in Fredericton. As we stood on the platform, we were surrounded by dark, coniferous woods, the type of rustic New Brunswick landscape that Dad loved to paint. The last thing Mum said was, "Remember, you can always come home."

I sat quietly in my seat as the train lumbered through forests and meadows. At dusk, a porter came along and made up my bed. There was a canvas curtain to pull across the bunk. I ate the big sloppy egg sandwich that Mum had made for me with her homemade brown bread and fell asleep to the train's gentle rocking.

The trip across Canada took five days. I loved the way the train pulled into stations big and small, some at 2:00 in the morning, all across the country. I loved going to the dining car where the tables were covered with white linen. I spent most of my time simply drifting in thought.

Lesley, my godsister, came to meet me at the train station in Vancouver wearing a baggy blue smock top and dirty jeans. Her crazy blonde hair was tied up at the back with clips and bobby pins and barrettes. We took a bus to the rundown brown stucco house she was renting in Marpole. Les was going to a college nearby, studying art and early childhood education. After a supper of canned brown beans, we sat in her living room on overstuffed maroon furniture covered in colourful Mexican blankets. At the end of the evening, she made a bed up for me on the couch.

The next morning, after Les had left for school, I ventured out to an area called the "West End." I took to the neighbourhood immediately. Pastel-coloured apartment buildings sat along beautiful English Bay, offering wonderful views out to sea. Concrete-arched bathing houses stood along one stretch of the beach. In the 1950s, before I was born, Mum had painted them standing stolidly under a grey sky; in front was my brother, four years old, in a red coat, feeding the pigeons clustered at his feet. Today, rusty red freighters were moored in the distance, and I followed a lovely seawall that ambled from the sandy beach into lush Stanley Park, which I discovered was full of trails, gardens, ponds and wildlife. There were swans, Canada geese and lily pads on Lost Lagoon, and I saw boats, totem poles and a zoo. Every so often, I came upon a hot-dog stand.

In the small zoo, two polar bears were confined in a cement pen surrounded by a tall iron fence. One lay by the side of a pool, but the other padded backwards around the pool the whole time I was there. It bothered me later, but I didn't think much of it then—I had my own life to establish.

The two main streets in the West End were crowded with cafés,

ENGLISH BAY

oil ☙ *Molly Lamb Bobak*

bookshops, ethnic eateries and funny little stores selling everything from surfboards to sex toys. As I cut down quiet Harwood Street, I saw an "Apartment for Rent" sign on the lawn in front of a low, rectangular building. The landlords were an older couple, somebody's grandparents, and the tiny apartment had a combined kitchen and living room, a bathroom and an alcove for a bed. The floors were hardwood. I took the place on the spot.

I moved from Les's house into my new beige apartment. I found a single bed with a lump in the mattress in a second-hand store a block away, bought a blue bicycle and got a library card. Every evening I rode my bike around the seawall, past the grey-bearded men on stools selling their oil paintings, alongside the dripping clay and sandstone cliffs with their green, red and yellow succulent plants growing in the crevices, past Siwash Rock and under the curved Lions Gate Bridge to the banging rhythm of traffic, then along a straight section with a view across Burrard Inlet of the docks and tankers and high piles of powdery yellow sulphur. North Vancouver rose slowly behind, up into the dark, treed mountains.

After a few weeks, I landed a job as a production assistant with a local theatre company based at the end of Davie Street. I did everything, including dressing the actors, and on one occasion, as I zipped the leading actress into her dress, a blue chiffon affair, I noticed that her back was covered in teeth marks. She'd come rushing in late that evening, as had the handsome leading man.

Davie Street was a bit raunchy in those days, lined with cheap family restaurants, tacky magazine shops, electronic outlets and massage parlours. It was also notorious for its hookers. I'd walk past it all every night after the theatre performances were over. I loved the activity under the red neon glow, the smell of greasy fast food and the old brick buildings with their fire escapes and bay windows. I'd turn onto a quiet, tree-lined street at the gay bookshop for my final few blocks home. Out in English Bay I could see the tankers looking quite fragile, lit up in the sea under the dark sky.

One day, as I was walking along Davie to the theatre, a man approached and asked if I would be interested in "working with a photographer." I could make some money doing it, he said. I shoved the card he gave me into my jeans pocket and continued on my way. I was curious, and a little flattered, so the next morning I called the photographer, whose name was Stan. He told me he had a studio in Marpole, and I agreed to meet him there the following afternoon.

Stan's studio was in a stucco building with a large front window. The office smelled musty. It was empty, so I sat down to wait on a black vinyl chair beside a rack of dated *Vogue* magazines. The room's ceiling was covered in little gold stars. After a few minutes, a tall, pretty woman walked out. She seemed very sure of herself in her tiny short skirt and gold belt. I felt rather plump in my jeans. I needed a haircut, and my nails were stained from painting the set for the next play. The man on the street had seemed to think I was worth photographing, though.

After another few minutes, a tall man with thinning dark hair came out drying his hands. "I'm Stan," he said. "What do you think of my Venus flytraps?" He motioned to some funny plants in the terrarium behind me.

Stan showed me around, beginning with his darkroom out back. We peeped into a bland brown bedroom, where there was an old dresser covered in wigs. Stan's wife liked to wear them, he said. Back out in the front room he showed me his portfolio, a beaten-up album with photos of sexy-looking girls he had taken for magazines. I must have the potential to be like those sexy girls, I thought, or I wouldn't be sitting in his office. Stan asked me to come back in a few days in nicer clothing and we would take some pictures.

I was excited when I got back to my Harwood apartment. I called Mum and Dad and told them that I had met a photographer who thought I had a lot of potential as a model. Dad said, "That's nice, but no nudies."

The next day I bought a pair of white jeans at the Bay, and a pair of gold-coloured earrings. I decided I'd diet a bit before I visited Stan again, but I was so hungry one night after a day of lettuce that I ate a whole Sara Lee cake. My photos could always be airbrushed, I figured.

I returned to Stan's musty office as planned, and we drove out to a dirty beach with a lot of industrial activity in the background. Stan told me to sit on a log, and he took pictures. I felt awkward, and my white jeans were getting dirty. When he developed the pictures later, back in the studio, I didn't look at all like the provocative models in his portfolio; I looked like a chubby girl sitting on a muddy log not really knowing what to do with her legs.

Stan gave me some tips on how to be more feminine. We chatted about life when I went to see him, and he took a few more shots here and there. One day, as we were talking, Stan went out and got a carton of eggs from the fridge he had out back. He did a weird, waving-hand motion over one egg, then placed the egg on the arborite table beside us. "Where's your earring?" he said. I checked, and my right, gold-coloured earring was missing. Stan cracked open the egg, and there it was. I was quite nonplussed by the whole event. And just then I saw the Venus flytrap catch a bug.

One day Stan draped me in a wig and blue clingy fabric, and, in smoky light, took some glamorous photos, which he sent to the *Daily Gleaner* in Fredericton. The paper published a shot of me in between two Great Dane dogs. Mum and Dad got a phone call about it from a heavy breather; they thought it was hilarious.

Mum came out to visit me in Vancouver in the autumn. We had souvlaki at a Greek place on the beach and walked the seawall. We went to Chinatown to buy paper lanterns and inexpensive white dishes with blue fish painted on them. We'd buy greens to eat for supper, and Mum would pick daisies from the lawn at English Bay and do little watercolours of them.

Of course I had to take her to meet Stan. I said to her on the bus, "Just wait until you see his amazing Venus flytraps." I wore my gold-coloured earrings, too, so that I could ask him to show Mum his trick.

Mum knew all about Marpole. She told me as we rode that when she was a girl, her father had had a farm nearby. Mum was born at Burnaby Lake but the family later moved to the area which was now Oak Street. Marpole was all fields and orchards then, and she and Gran would take the streetcar into Vancouver. Gran shopped at a butcher shop called "We Have Meat That Ye Can Eat."

When we got to Stan's studio, I sat Mum down on a black vinyl chair. The first thing I said to her, with breathless excitement, was, "Look at the gold stars on the ceiling."

Stan came out, and I asked him to do the egg trick. He waved his hands over a single egg he'd set on an old Vogue magazine and then said, "Where's your earring?"

He cracked the egg and the yolk dripped all over the magazine. My earrings were still in my ears.

"Show Mum your Venus flytraps," I said. We looked in the terrarium, and the plants were all closed up asleep.

Mum and I took the bus back to my apartment. After I'd made a cup of tea, we walked the sand on English Bay, watching as the freighters in the harbour lit up one by one. On the way home, we passed the men selling their oil paintings of orange Stanley Park sunsets and sailboats on a turquoise sea.

the comb

WHEN I WAS IN MY early 20s, after a long recovery from scarlet fever, I left Vancouver and went to England for a change of scenery. I stayed at first with my Uncle Abby, one of Mum's half-brothers, and his wife, Irene. They lived in a white cottage trimmed in the traditional black-painted beams in a village called Birdham, near Chichester.

It was a lovely area, and Irene and I took a brisk walk together every day. She wore skirts and thick beige nylons and brown leather shoes, and she would take great strides, almost leaping over the stiles that led to narrow paths along the edges of farmers' fields. We walked through bluebell woods and masses of yellow rapeseed, through orchards, down shady lanes lined with beech trees, and over sturdy stone bridges that crossed babbling brooks.

We had a roast on Sundays after Abby came home from the small church down the road where he was the minister. While Abby and Irene had their pre-dinner sherry in the front sitting room, I sat in a floral wingback chair and wrote to Mum. After our meal, if the weather was nice, we read the Sunday papers outside, in Abby's rose garden. Staying with Abby and Irene was conventional and comforting, just what I needed at the time. No matter what happened, roast would be served, with potatoes and peas, on Sunday.

I was hoping to work in England for a while, and soon I got a job as a groom at a polo stable in a nearby village called Bosham. I was supposed to work with a few other girls, exercising the club owner's ponies, and part of the deal was that I could live in the house he had rented for his grooms. Well—those English girls were as hard as nails. They had thighs of steel, for one thing. I had been riding horses all my life, but I could barely handle the six hours a day of trotting a horse steadily up and down hills on pavement while leading two other ponies. My thighs were raw and my hands developed blisters. The other grooms resented me, and they were always putting me down.

Things weren't any better on the home front. The girls lived in squalor. Their house was filthy, and they drank beer and slept with local rock musicians who would come and go all night. I slept alone in a sleeping bag on the floor of an empty room with a grungy olive-green carpet.

One afternoon at the polo stable, I met a wealthy man who lived on an estate on the edge of the village. He needed a nanny for his two young children, he told me, because his wife found it too difficult to cope with their big house and all the entertaining. It turned out they were Canadians too; he was some kind of adviser to the Canadian government.

The man hired me, and I moved into a lovely, bright room in their grand sandstone home, with its spiral staircases and chandeliers, gardens and stables and chefs and housekeepers. I looked after the children, but the person who really needed help was the man's wife. The family had two nice horses, but the woman, who dressed in canary-coloured jodhpurs and leather boots, was terrified of riding. She and I went on a few anxious trail rides. At night, as I lay in my room, I could hear her wailing upstairs.

After I'd been a nanny for a month or two, I saw an ad in the local paper for a position with a community theatre company called "Word and Action." The company was based in the village of Cole Hill, just next to the seaside town of Bournemouth in Dorset. A week later, on my afternoon off, I took the train to a grotty little station and waited on the street for a man named Greg to pick me up; the troupe had invited me to stay for the weekend to meet everyone and to get the feel of their philosophy.

Greg, the company's founder, was a large man in his 50s, with a bit of a stoop and very bowed legs. As we drove to Cole Hill, he explained that the company had rented a house to use as an office, and that the three members of the acting group—Liz, Peter and Greg himself—lived upstairs. That's where I would be staying. They were all vegetarians, he said, and they shared the household duties. I assured him I liked to garden and to clean.

I loved the house instantly. The large windows on the front overlooked a garden lush with tangled grass and a lovely mature fig tree. Beyond was a view of Bournemouth and the sea. Greg's mate, Liz, was waiting for us inside. She was friendly and plump and a bit bedraggled. After a cup of tea under the fig tree, Greg led me to the office. He explained that the company performed in schools, and that their technique combined the words students gave them with actions reflecting the students' words and thoughts. They had many contracts in Europe, he said, because the method was a good tool for teaching English.

Greg sat me down and asked me to read a letter sent to Word and Action by a Danish school district. He said it would be a good test of whether or not I was suitable for the job, so I read the letter slowly, not to miss a thing. When I came to the part that read, "Thank yu for all yoor effarts. We luk forwerd to metting yu soon. I will mail the sined shits to you today," I burst out laughing. Greg's face was red from containing his own laughter, and he said I had passed the test. Would I be willing to take the job and move in within a week? I took the train back to Chichester to pack my bags.

My new room in Cole Hill had a slanted ceiling and a view over the back garden. The company was set to depart on a European tour soon, and until then we did plays and skits at local schools, old peoples' homes, community centres and pub gardens. We all shared in both the administrative duties and the acting. I bought an old green bike from a junk man in the village and biked into Bournemouth on my days off.

Greg and Liz cooked enormous vegetarian meals. Greg would carry in a platter with a cauliflower in the centre, surrounded by chunks of cooked carrots and other root vegetables, all covered in a thick cheese sauce. Big bowls of salads followed. My food-related job was to garden. I picked figs and planted lettuces and weeded out the garden's stone wall.

Denmark was the first stop on Word and Action's theatre tour. Greg, Liz, Peter and I took an overnight ferry to Denmark. I was booked into a single bunk with a shared bathroom down the corridor. Before I turned in I had three Irish coffees in the lounge. I slept in my red sweatshirt and jeans. The next morning we drove the company's white Cortina through the flat green countryside. It took two more ferries to get to the island where our host, Arne, lived. Arne turned out to be a friendly, happy man with a big, balding head. His place would be our base for the next few days.

By a strange coincidence, Mum was scheduled to fly into Copenhagen later that week on some kind of Canadian/Danish art venture. Greg, Liz, Peter and I did a school production in town, then picked Mum up in the afternoon. On the ferry back to Arne's island, Mum and I sat out on the deck. Everything was painted bright enamelled white, and the red-crossed Danish flag fluttered off the stern.

Greg made supper that night, bringing in a big platter of vegetables covered in his trademark sauce. Mum had bought some wine at the ferry terminal, but Liz wouldn't drink any because she was trying to have a baby and had already had three miscarriages.

After supper, Mum and I went for a walk to spend some time alone. It had been raining, and the dark road was damp. The tall limbs

of the trees were black against the light-grey sky, just ready for the moon to appear. The few houses we passed were whitewashed, with freshly painted black shutters and low shake roofs.

Suddenly Mum stooped in excitement and picked something up from the gravel. "Look at this," she said. "A comb! I forgot mine in Fredericton—it's just what I need!" She put it in her coat pocket.

Mum is very lucky at finding things. She spots coins in the grass along the riverbank near her house, and one time, when she'd seen a five-dollar bill blowing across the Burrard Bridge in Vancouver amongst the grit and the litter and the cars, I'd chased it down. And then she'd yelled, "There goes a 10!" but it blew under the wheels of the traffic.

When we got back to Arne's house, Greg was reading in the living room under a lamp with a rice-paper shade. Liz and Arne had gone to bed. Mum and I were sharing a room in Arne's loft, where he'd made up two futons with crisp, blue-and-white-striped cotton sheets. Before we went to sleep, Mum washed her comb in the sink. She still has that comb, and she carries it with her whenever she visits me on Glamorgan Farm.

I stayed with Word and Action for the next two years, travelling all over Sweden, France, Belgium and Italy. The two best places were Naples and Venice. But finally I got homesick for Canada's west coast, and I returned with a large load of luggage and a bag of Bath Olivers, a bland biscuit I had come to adore.

the photo album

MUM AND I TALK ABOUT all kinds of things after supper, by the fire, when she's visiting me on Glamorgan Farm. Some nights I bring down a musty old photo album of hers. The faded photographs glued onto the black paper show Mum as a baby and a toddler at Burnaby Lake, where she grew up, in her pram or sitting on the grass on her family's farm, or, wobbly, standing in a white smock and bonnet grabbing Gran's leg. There is one of her under a tree with her lap full of little white puppies from her dog, Emma, and another that shows chubby blonde Mum standing beside her Jersey cow, the two of them looking rather alike.

Every time we go through the album, Mum says, as she turns a certain page, "Oh, look, there's dear Abby. He was always so nervous." Abby, one of her half-brothers, was the runt of the family. Mum had three other half-brothers, too.

Mum's father, Harold Mortimer-Lamb, had come from England as a young man, settling in Port Moody, B.C., because it was the last train stop on the line. That would have been around 1885, about 15 years after Glamorgan Farm was established by its first owner, a Welshman named Richard John.

Young Harold first hired himself out as a farm hand, but he ran away from a farmer who worked him too hard, and he became a lay reader with the Anglican Church in a parish near Chilliwack. When he lost faith in religion, he started a newspaper. He married a girl named Kate, and they had six children, two of whom died in childhood.

At some point, Harold and Kate and their children ended up in Montreal, and hired a woman to help with the family. This was Mary Price, my Gran, who happened to be running a hand laundry at the time. Gran had also come from England, from Canterbury. She'd settled first in St. Andrews, New Brunswick, where she had taken a job as the gardener at a seaside estate. Gran was always restless, and she never stayed long in one place. (Later, on Galiano Island, she'd move house every few years, after she'd cleaned each one up and established a beautiful garden.) So she soon moved west to Montreal. One of her best friends there was Kathleen Shackleton, sister of the famous Antarctic explorer.

Eventually, Gran took over the Mortimer-Lamb household, looking after the boys, and Kate too. The family moved back to Burnaby, and my mother was born soon afterwards, to Gran. Kate ended up being called "Gombo," short for godmother. Harold, who'd had a nervous breakdown, took to farming to calm himself. Harold and Gran never married, and she finally went off to find a life of her own. I don't know what happened to Kate, who, Mum says, used to sit in a red chair in the family's Burnaby Lake parlour and say, "Trouble, trouble, trouble," over and over again.

Harold became a well-known photographer, and he was a friend to many artists. He helped some of them, including Emily Carr, although Mum says that Harold and Emily had wicked fights. One of Harold's friends, Fred Varley, who taught at the Vancouver School of Art, had a prize student named Vera Weatherby, who ending up marrying Harold. Gran apparently encouraged the marriage.

Mum often tells the story of how she learned that her father had married Vera. "I went home to Burnaby Lake one night in 1942, after I had been accepted into the Canadian army as a war artist. There was a faint light on in the house, but all the doors were locked, which was quite unusual. I crawled through the bushes to a window and climbed in. Dadda and Vera were sitting on the sofa in the living room by the fire. I was surprised to see them there together. And then Vera said, in her bird-like way, 'Your father and I were married today. I hope you don't mind.' I was rather shocked and felt quite alone."

I remember being taken to visit Harold several times by Mum when he was very old and feeble. Vera drove an old blue Austin, and she would pick Mum and me up at a bus stop on a pleasant street in Burnaby. Vera and Harold lived at the top of a long, narrow lane. Their house was cozy, with lots of Persian rugs and Oriental vases and pottery and overstuffed furniture, and windows with big views out to Vancouver. Harold was bedridden by this time, and we would go to see him in his bedroom. Mum would hug and kiss him, but I held back when he reached his pale, thin arms out to me. He was a tiny, tiny man sunk in amongst billowing white pillows and duvets. Vera always let me go outdoors, and the thing I loved most was making my way down an overgrown path between rhododendrons to a pond full of goldfish. Vera's dog, Abby, would follow me.

After Harold died, Vera stayed on in the house. Later, when I moved to Vancouver and was living in a small beige apartment near English Bay, I would take the bus out to visit her. Every time I saw her, she seemed smaller. She'd greet me at the door wearing a big turtleneck sweater that made her neck look even tinier. Her grey hair was always in a bun, which she held in place with long pins. One day, as we walked through the kitchen, she said in her nervous way, "Don't go near the stove—the devil's in the oven," so I never did.

Vera died a year or so after that, when I was very ill with scarlet fever and confined to my apartment. Mum was taking care of me, and she answered the phone when Hal, one of her older brothers, called with the news. I was still weak, but a few days later Mum bundled me up in a Cowichan sweater and Hal's wife took us to Vera's house. It was Mum's job to sort through the contents and handle some aspects of the will.

Harold and Vera had left much of their art collection to the Art Gallery of Greater Victoria. I lay on their plush green sofa for the last time as Mum reviewed the collection with a man in a suit. Vera's will said I could choose two items of theirs to keep, so I selected four white plates with pink roses painted on them and Harold's eiderdown, which I use to this day on my brass bed on Glamorgan Farm.

Harold and Vera's own paintings—many of them of each other and of their Burnaby Mountain home—were unclaimed, and I took them back to my apartment. The best one, I think, is of Vera. Harold depicted her pushing a small, elegant table; she's wearing a red sweater that clings to her narrow torso. I have it hanging on a white wall upstairs, beside a photograph that Harold took of Gran shucking peas.

There's another story Mum always tells when we look through her photo album. One of her half-brothers, Lawrence—Mum called him "Law"—lived in Vancouver and had a wife named Ruth. They were very proper. Uncle Law worked in a bank, and every day he walked to the bus from their white stucco house near Granville Street with his briefcase, and a devilled-egg sandwich in his coat pocket. He died when I was about 13, but Ruth lived much longer.

After Uncle Law died, she became a little more adventurous, and she and Mum went to Scotland together. Before that, Ruth had never travelled anywhere. They went up north to Oban, a little town on the rugged west coast, and stayed in a hotel on the water's edge. The radiator didn't work, and it was so cold that they had to share a bed. In the middle of the night, as Mum tells it, Ruth, in her prim English accent, asked in a weak voice, "Molly, what do *lesbians* do?"

And there are always lots of funny stories to remember about Gran. Mum is particularly fond of one that involves a painting. After Mum had grown and gone off to art school, Gran decided she'd had enough of living with Harold and taking care of his home. She moved out to a beautiful property on Galiano Island called Arbutus Point, where she ran a summer resort in a large red shake-and-shingle house. Her front lawn merged into a sloping sandstone beach right on Active Pass. The dark-green water churned as the ferries passed through.

Harold set Gran up very nicely, and when she left him at Burnaby Lake she took with her a little oil painting, a Quebec winter scene, painted around that time by Harold's friend, A.Y. Jackson, a prominent member of the Group of Seven. The painting was of a barren field. In the distance were bleak purple winter hills, and in the foreground a few scrubby evergreens and grasses cast dark-blue shadows on the dusky light of the snow.

Gran was someone who never cared about value or money. At some point she needed a rug for her hallway at the resort, and she traded the A.Y. Jackson for what Mum recalls as "a threadbare, ugly old mat." A few years later, Harold wanted the painting back for an exhibition. Gran panicked! She called Mum and said, "What should I do?"

Uncle A.Y., as I called him when I was a child, was a family friend, and Mum bailed Gran out by asking him to paint the picture over again—Harold would never know. Kind A.Y. remembered the painting, and he agreed to redo it. To Mum's eyes, it looked identical but when she delivered it to Harold, he took one look at it and said, "This is not the same painting at all. This was painted recently, and my original was done in 1920."

The replica now hangs in my living room above the fireplace, beside a picture done for me by a Belarussian orphan of cows grazing in a yellow meadow. In front of the fire is Gran's old tattered mat, where the dogs like to lie after a long walk through the woods.

VERA WITH FLOWERS
oil ❧ Harold Mortimer-Lamb

a s h e s

GRAN AND UNK SPENT MANY happy years together on Galiano Island. They both loved the place, and they delighted in recounting funny episodes from their time there. Some of their stories were clearly exaggerated, but they were very entertaining.

One story, for example, had it that, on a dark and freezing winter night, Gran and Unk went outside and shot their gun into the air to scare off the neighbour's loose and wandering horses. At dawn, Unk went out to gather a load of wood, only to see two dead horses lying in Gran's garden. In a panic, he dug a shallow grave in the frozen earth (maybe he had a backhoe) and they rolled the horses into the hole with ropes. Because the animals were frozen, though, their legs stuck up straight and couldn't be covered. According to the story, Gran sawed them off.

When Gran and Unk got so old they needed help, they moved to an apartment in a seniors' complex on Saltspring Island. Gran planted

Canterbury bells, asters and poppies on their patio. When Mum and I visited them from New Brunswick, we stayed in single beds in the main building, which sat on a slope overlooking Ganges Harbour.

One evening, after Mum and I had said our usual goodnight to Gran and Unk, Mum stopped off at the bathroom down the hall and I continued on to our room. In my bed was an old lady, snoring her head off. She had grey curly hair and was wearing a red satin dressing-gown. I was shocked, and I ran out of the room to get Mum. I met her in the hall. She laughed and explained that the old lady was simply lost and confused. She went to get the supervisor, who gently took the lady back to her own room.

In Fredericton, we lived in an old Loyalist house painted pale yellow with white trim. The house had a spacious, musty attic with high wooden beams and small windows in the turrets, which Mum used as her studio. She loved to paint crowd scenes, and I remember one painting of the winter parade down Queen Street, all the coloured woollen caps, boots and waving mittened arms of the crowd that lined the snowy street under a faded yellow winter sky. Red-brick heritage buildings lined the route on one side, with the Metropolitan store, Vandine's shoe shop and the Victory Meat Market across the way.

Another painting I remember was one of the patients at Fredericton's new Chalmers Hospital. The hospital had been built up on the hill above the university in a barren field; it was a huge white box with yellow trim and aluminum vents that spewed steam and the smell of stale dinners into the snow. Mum's painting showed a group of patients in bathrobes and faded pink slippers sitting in wheelchairs, IVs hanging above them, smoking in the hospital parking lot in the dead cold of a Fredericton winter. She called it *Life and Death*.

Our house was large. Red and gold Moroccan rugs covered the wood floors, and in the living room, light came in through pale mauve and green stained-glass windows. The walls were covered in my parents' paintings. Dad was producing huge oils of nude figures at the time, with gobs of paint hanging off the faces and pudgy bodies of men in gymnasium showers or the soft bodies of women under cherry trees laden with fruit. Dad often found antique wooden furniture in abandoned farmhouses around the New Brunswick countryside, and he'd bring it home to be stripped and varnished.

Mum and Dad entertained regularly, giving lively, fun parties with their university friends—musicians and other artists and historians, English academics and classical scholars. As I lay in my bed upstairs I could hear the laughing and carrying-on downstairs late into the evening.

One night, during one of those parties, I heard the telephone ring. A few minutes later Mum ran up the wooden staircase, and then I heard her in her room, crying loudly. It sounded as if somebody else was with her. I felt very empty, hearing Mum cry like that. I could still hear the cheerful chatting, clinking glasses, baroque music playing on the hi-fi and the metal serving spoons dishing out salads and cabbage rolls from clay bowls.

Mum told me the next morning that Gran had died of a stroke in their apartment on Saltspring. She had said to Unk, "Jack, get me my pills. I have a pain in my chest," and when Unk came back from the bedroom into the living room, where they'd been watching "Hockey Night in Canada"—Gran's favourite team was the Toronto Maple Leafs, and she always talked about Phil Esposito—she was dead.

Mum and my older brother Sasha flew out to the west coast to deal with things. Gran was cremated at a funeral home on Saltspring, but she had always told Mum she wished to have her ashes scattered in Active Pass. The funeral-home man handed Mum the plastic bag.

Mum and Sasha took the small white ferry with the royal-blue funnel over to Galiano Island. They went to the little graveyard there, which is on a high sandstone cliff, surrounded by drooping cedars and firs, with wild daisies and tiny sweet red strawberries pushing through the moss and grasses. Below are the turbulent green swirls and currents of the pass. Sea lions lounge on the rocks at low tide.

I'd been in the graveyard many times myself. One summer when Mum and I were staying with Gran on Galiano, there was great excitement on a cool morning: a Russian freighter on its way to Vancouver had gone aground on the shallow rocks below the graveyard. The impact had caused a grand shudder in all the local cottages. Gran and I rushed to the cliff. Mum grabbed her sketchbook and charcoal pencils and scrambled down to the shore to draw the great drama.

In later years, some of the people I loved would be buried in that graveyard as well. My old friend Hoppy—short for Elizabeth Hopkins— has a brown headstone in a shady corner. She lived on Galiano for

ROLLING PASTURES

oil ☙ Bruno Bobak

many years, and became famous as an artist when she was 84. Hoppy had a large cat named The Colonel, and she used to give guests of any age Bloody Marys and peanuts when they visited her. The children who knew her left ceramic animals (the kind found in tea boxes), white shells and pebbles at the spot. Yarah, my goddaughter, is also buried there. She died at age 17 on Saltspring Island; she drove around a dark corner late one night and went into the lake.

That afternoon, Mum and Sasha walked to the edge of the cliff with the plastic bag the funeral director had handed them. Mum opened the bag and tossed the contents into the sea, but rather than ashes, out came Gran's red cardigan and a blue woollen skirt! Mum remembers seeing the clothes floating through the air, then down over the cliff. She watched until the sea took them under.

I asked Mum, one night when she was visiting, who bought the painting that she called *Life and Death*. She couldn't remember, but she said that she had known one of the women sitting in a wheelchair, smoking. The woman, she said, had weak knees, so her husband had built an elevator in their house. The woman had fallen down the shaft and broken both her ankles; that's why she was in the hospital.

"That's one thing we don't have to worry about," said Mum. "We have good bones. Not very good nerves, and absolutely no memory, but good bones, and I still have all my teeth. They're filthy, mind you, not a good colour, but still there."

two for one

ONE SUMMER AFTERNOON MY FRIEND Lorna called, and after chatting for a while, we decided we'd visit the SPCA. A week earlier I'd had to put down my wonderful dog Havel (named after the Czech prime minister and playwright) and I was very sad about losing him.

Havel was a handsome, golden-coloured, muscular dog with a bulldog face I had adopted from the SPCA years earlier. He talked when he was happy, with a joyous, wailing howl, showing his pink gums and gleaming teeth. He was kind to all creatures, and a loyal friend. When Mum visited he would walk cautiously beside her around the farm; he seemed to know intuitively that her sight was failing. But his hips had finally given out after years of romping through the woods and leaping into winter-storm waves to retrieve logs. I'd buried him up at the back of the property, under a huge, drooping cedar.

When I arrived to pick Lorna up, she was out in her garden; her partner, Patrick, was reading in a green-painted wooden lawn chair under a gnarled apple tree. I'd brought along my three dogs, Baby Alice Mary, Daisy and Lily, in case I found a new farm dog I wanted them to meet.

The traffic was heavy in the strip-mall suburb going into town. We passed the bowling alley and the car dealerships with their strings of silver and red flags. Lorna commented on how funny the new Smart cars looked. "They look as if they should be driven by dogs!" she said.

When we arrived at the SPCA, we went inside to look at the row of dogs up for adoption. There was a tan pit bull named Logan. His tag read, "I am happy and LOVE cats and belly rubs." Under that, in red letters, it said, "I snap at children." We kept going. There was an old beagle who "needed a fenced yard," and a lovely, big, friendly dog named Emily whose tag said, "I kill cats." We decided to leave and try again another day.

But, "Let's look at the cats before we go," said Lorna.

The SPCA people directed us to two grey rooms full of clean kennels, each with a blanket and a sleeping box and a mouse toy, and a cat asleep inside. There were cats of all shapes, colours and sizes. A huge, furry, grey Persian shared her kennel with a slim ginger cat: "Bonded Pair," their tag read. Above the kennels were perches and carpeted platforms, all full of lounging cats. Sometimes we could see only a tail hanging down, or a paw. In a glassed-in room called "the cat communal area," at least 30 cats were loose. As we walked in, a white paw reached up for a black tail above.

In a corner of the communal area, on a ripped green vinyl ottoman, sat an old, black-and-white cat with a sagging belly and a large head. His nose was white but he had a black smudge over his mouth.

"Look at that poor thing," Lorna said. "Has he has just come out of a world war?" I went over to the old cat and he stared me right in the eye. As soon as I sat down, he crawled up onto my lap and settled down for a nap. His little blue plastic collar read "Peter."

Lorna and I went into the office to ask about Peter's history. A young woman in tight jeans with a hundred earrings in one ear looked up his file. Peter's family had given him up because they were moving. He had been at the SPCA for months and was showing signs of stress, the young woman said. Nobody had ever asked about him.

We went back to see Peter in the little glass room and there he was, still sitting on his ottoman. I decided to take him. Just as I was filling out the papers back in the office, an SPCA volunteer came in with a huge, grizzled, black-and-white dog. "You want that old dog too?" asked the young woman. "He's just come in from a walk. We rescued him this morning from a drug house."

I bent down to see him, and it was love at first sight. Within five minutes, Lorna had named the dog Fernando and he was in the back of my van with Baby Alice Mary. Daisy and Lily sat on the seat in front, like two ladies going to the opera. We'd agreed that I would come back the next day for Peter.

When I got home, I helped Fernando out of the van. He came into the kitchen, a bit blasé, as if he had seen it all before, then lay down on a rug by the stove and fell fast asleep. Four of the seven cats walked unperturbed over his gangly body to get to their dinner on the pantry counter. (I have to feed them up there or Baby Alice Mary will scoff their food.)

The next morning the SPCA called to say that Peter had been taken to the sick room; they would call again when he was well enough to be picked up. Lorna and I decided to take the dogs for a walk at Blue Heron Park. They trotted around for a while, meeting other dogs, sniffing fence posts and panting with joy. Fernando headed off in another direction. When he was oblivious to our calling, we realized he was probably deaf.

In a lovely marsh full of bulrushes and yellow water iris, the dogs had a sloppy drink. We walked through some pastoral trails lined with wild currant, salmonberry and willows, then into the cedar woods. Fernando panted heavily but followed slowly behind.

Lorna and I speculated about what it meant for an animal's spirit to be broken. Then we wondered what it meant for a person's spirit to be broken. I dropped her off after our walk and took the dogs home. All of us went up to bed early that night, after I'd locked in the chickens and ducks, checked on Mabel and Matilda, and let the horses out into their back paddock.

A few days later the SPCA called to say that Peter was out of the sick room. I stopped by to pick up Lorna, and off we went with my blue plastic cat-carrying case in the van, back past the strip malls and car dealerships to the SPCA. I went to the cat communal area and there was sweet Peter, back sitting on his green vinyl ottoman. He went into my cage with great ease. I finished the paperwork and then took Peter out to the car. He sat quietly in the cage in the back seat, taking everything in stride.

When we got back to Glamorgan Farm, Lorna gave Peter the cat treats she had brought, and I carried him upstairs so he could spend some time alone settling in. In Mum's room I had placed a pan of fresh kitty litter and a small dish of hard food. Lorna and I assumed Peter would be stressed but instead, he cautiously exited his cage. I gave him a spoonful of canned food, and he loved it! Then he jumped stiffly up on Mum's dresser and went to sleep on Gran's red Hudson's Bay blanket.

The other cats met Peter later that evening with a calm, friendly interest. Peter accepted the dogs in the same way. By my bath time he was downstairs, and by bedtime he was sitting out on the deck, taking in the evening country air. When I went up to bed, Peter came too, and scrambled up onto the bed to lie beside me. Fernando slept beside the bed on his blue rug.

As I drifted off, I felt Peter's scrawny paw on my wrist and heard Fernando's contented snore. Outside, the frogs in the nearby pond had begun their nighttime chorus.

coming along

THERE IS A SHOP IN Sidney where I take pictures to be framed. It
is right on the main street, next to a restaurant that serves homemade
chocolates and breads. In the window of the framing shop there are
art posters elegantly framed, using non-glare glass and double mats.
Inside, on the counter, sits a large binder with mat samples in a mul-
titude of colours and thicknesses. The walls are covered with frame
samples and mirrors and Persian rugs framed to perfection. Coloured
glass balls, cards of local scenes, copper and brass lanterns, scented
candles, Arabian ornaments, silk embroideries from Asia and amber
enamelled dishware are all displayed for sale.

The shop has recently come under new ownership, and the new
framer is an efficient Englishman who dresses in khaki cotton trou-
sers and short-sleeved plaid shirts. His soft-spoken wife looks after
the customers; she has thick dark hair and a kind, serene face.

One day I took in a watercolour of North Saanich wildflowers to

WILD FLOWERS AND WILD IRIS
watercolour   *Molly Lamb Bobak*

be framed—a simple white double mat and thin gold-plated wooden frame would be perfect. Mum had done it a year or two earlier at my kitchen table. We had picked the flowers in an overgrown field behind the racetrack—daisies, buttercups, clover, poppies, Queen Anne's Lace, white apple blossoms from a gnarled old tree and some wild iris.

The framing shop was my first stop, to be followed by a haircut at Olga's, just around the corner, and the purchase of some pantyhose at the lingerie shop across the street. I needed some sheer charcoal hose for the upcoming municipal election campaign, something that would go with a pin-striped skirt and white blouse.

The woman at the framing shop took the watercolour from me and then said, in her soothing voice, "Please, take some cards—a gift from me to you." She insisted, so I chose an Emily Carr reproduction of a forest with swirling trees, in deep greens and browns. A day or two later, I took her a dozen freshly laid eggs. I included a sprig of lovage, a favourite herb of mine and one that goes very well with eggs.

When I picked up the watercolour a couple of weeks later, there was a new young assistant in the shop. She retrieved the painting from the back shelf, and we inspected it on the counter. The frame looked exquisite. The young clerk gushed over the art, and I told her my mother had done it. "Oh," said the clerk, "my mother paints, too. Your mother is really coming along, isn't she?"

Mum roared when I told her the story. I hung her *Wild Flowers and Wild Iris* up in my bedroom, next to the framed photograph of me eating a frankfurter in New York.

arranging a still life

WHEN MUM'S EYES WERE BETTER, she would always do little watercolours of wildflowers at my kitchen table when she came to visit. One night by the fire, she was reminiscing about her early days at art school in Vancouver.

"The first year," she explained, "we learned how to draw and how to paint a still life. Oh, it was so formal. The teacher, a lovely old Scot, arranged the drapery and the objects, some apples or a vase, and then he placed spotlights on the arrangement to strategically create shadow. We all had easels, and Bert Binning (later a well-known painter and architect) would come in dressed as a baby in a pink bonnet and pretend to set up the still life and then knock it all down!

"We had to learn perspective, too, and we were told to hold one arm out at full length with our thumb up, to measure proportion. None of us really understood why we were doing that—it was just something an artist did before beginning a painting.

"Of course, a real still life should be haphazard," Mum concluded.

I looked around my living room. My rugs were scattered every which way, candles were dripping onto the table, and the tarnished tea service my granddad Harold had left me needed polishing. There was an inch of dust on the piano.

Mum's still lifes in my living room hang on the high white plaster walls. One is of a delicate white cyclamen on a dark table in front of a yellow curtain. I have one of Harold's too—little mauve daisies in his jade jug, a few apples at its base and a green bowl in the background. Dad's large still life, an oil in red and gold and rust—shades of flowers from his garden—hangs slightly crooked on the wall, with a cobweb across the top of its gold frame.

Here are Mum and Dad's instructions on how to set up a still life:

1.   Dad says that the objects in a still life must have a special meaning for the artist, perhaps reflecting a memory, a love for a certain item or feelings for a friend.

2.   Mum and Dad agree the still life should have a central focus—a special vase or flower, for example—even when the painting contains a number of objects.

3.   The artist must decide whether the still life will have a horizontal structure, or a vertical one. This is something Mum's old Scot would teach his class.

4.   Dad suggests choosing objects such as bowls, fruit or flowers that go well together in colour and shape. But he adds, "Of course,

a still life can be spontaneous—the artist could see something and say, 'Wow, that would make a great painting!' Such as our friend Joe Plaskett's painting of his dinner table the morning after: his dirty tablecloth, wine bottle and goblets, a pewter plate of grapes and a bouquet of fading tulips in the centre."

Mum agrees. "Sometimes you don't need to set up the balance—it's already there. A good artist can walk into a room and ask, 'How does that green bowl of pears sit in that ray of light against the plum sofa?' The artist will pick the form from observation and just let things happen. But it takes great skill, and courage, to march to your own drum like that, to go beyond what one learns, to go beyond the academic structure."

FLOWERS FROM BRUNO'S GARDEN
oil ✒ *Bruno Bobak*

the psychic

IT WAS THE HEIGHT OF summer, and a thick, soupy humidity had set in. The farm was dry. The poppies and marigolds had gone to seed, and the lawn had turned brown. Spindly nettle stems were higher than my head. There was a faint smell of blackberries mixed in with the dust, and the sky was a white haze.

The piggies enjoyed a cooling hosing-off at midday when I went out to give them their apples. The horses hung their heads lazily in the shade of a pine tree in the corner of their field. The ducks slept in their shed in the afternoons, and the chickens scratched out shallow holes in the soil for dust baths. The dogs moped around, spending most of their time under the honeysuckle, and the cats retreated to the damp areas beneath the house, coming out only at dusk when the light began to fade.

The oppressive air took away everybody's energy, and the heat went on day after day. I drove into Sidney and bought a deck chair and a patio umbrella at the hardware store. I sat out on the deck and read philosophy as the days drifted by. The chard went to seed in a bulbous mass of white flowers. Every so often I would rouse myself to shuck a few broad beans.

One day, for something to do, I went into town to see a psychic. Her ad in the local paper said she had worked for the police, and I suppose I was hoping she would tell me that luck was to come my way, that life would be happier soon, that success was just around the corner.

The psychic's name was Tammy. She lived on a short street in a blue house with a white railing around the deck. I went up some stone steps through a wild garden dotted with ceramic creatures, birdbaths and birdhouses. "Come in," she called from the cluttered deck.

Tammy wore tight jeans and a snug, lime-green tank top. Her tanned but pudgy midriff showed in between. She had long, dyed-blonde hair and was barefoot, with calloused heels and worn-off red toenail polish. She looked a bit weathered, but her manner was gentle—the heat was drying us all to a husk.

We chatted in her living room. Her boyfriend had dumped her, she said, and her 40-year-old son, who lived with her, had just lost his job and crashed their car. Tammy lit a cigarette as I settled into a cozy brown chair. The mirrors on the wall had gold star stickers around the edges, and the rug was a mustard-coloured shag. I felt guilty for thinking it, but I had assumed that a good psychic would also have very good taste, and now I was wondering.

Tammy sat across from me on a brown couch with red silk cushions, leafing through a box of yellowed cards. She used the cards to make her spiritual connections, she said. She started by saying that I was run down and needed a good six months to rest. I had something called "Candida," she said, a yeast condition in the intestine also known as "leaky gut." It made me almost sick to hear her describe it. She said too that my star was rising and that by the New Year I would have much success—my book would win an award, I would top the polls in the November municipal election and I would meet some new close friends, including one named Christine who "worked for the community."

"Don't call her Chris," Tammy warned, "and don't come on too strong."

This was intriguing!

"An attractive woman in a blue truck will come down your driveway," she continued. "An inspector or someone, and the two of you will be kindred spirits. Things will get better for you when you become well. You will 'smell like a rose' in politics. You will become mayor in the next term and will wear a white blouse with a little embroidery on the collar." Then she sat up straight and said, "I'm tired—can't do any more."

I wrote Tammy a cheque and headed back out into the white, humid haze. I felt quite positive as I drove home along the highway. I had a quiet burst of energy in the days that followed, cleaning the house room by room, buying yeast-free groceries and weeding the garden. In between, I took naps on the deck.

The following week, I decided to call an engineer to look at my big barn. I wanted to bring it up to code so that I could hold fundraisers and readings in it in the autumn. The inspector, a pretty woman, drove up in a blue truck and gave me advice on the barn doors and stairs.

The next day, a woman named Christine called. She was a horticultural therapist who wanted to bring a group of gardeners to look at the Healthy Harvest Co-op's garden. After our conversation, I went back out to the deck, where I lay planning what I would say to Oprah when I was on her show after winning the book award. All the free breakfasts and power lunches when I was elected mayor would be fun too.

f e d R e x

I HAD ALWAYS WANTED TO visit Saskatoon—Mum says it's one of
her favourite places, because the people are so honest—so I flew there
for a weekend a while back and stayed in a lovely old hotel on the river.
It was a very pleasant break.

I took a taxi home from the airport, as usual, and as we came to a
stop on the farm's gravel driveway, I could see Gavin squatting in his
herb patch, just as he had been when I left. Annabel, the calico barn
cat, was sitting in the blackberries. The Old Gals came running out
on their short legs to greet me. Baby Alice Mary swaggered behind,
flashing me a great, pink-tongued grin. Fernando was probably asleep
on the kitchen floor, I thought. But he was nowhere to be seen when I
put down my pack inside.

The Old Gals and Alice had followed me in, wagging their tails.
When Peter and the other cats—Jimmy, Sweet, Willy, Pudge, Little
Bee and Miss Kitty—came into the kitchen a moment later, we were

all gathered in our little group. But where was Fernando? I went up-stairs to my room, but he was not there.

Gavin had been making his way slowly up to the house. When I stepped out onto the porch, he told me, "When I came to feed the dogs this morning, Fernando was gone. I've looked everywhere but he hasn't turned up."

Maybe Fernando had gone to die under a bush somewhere, I thought sadly. I walked around the farm, searching under every shed and clump of undergrowth I could see. My socks were covered in burrs and the sticky seeds of spear grass by the end, but there was still no sign of Fernando.

Nobody at the racetrack had seen Fernando, although they all asked after Alice Mary, who was a frequent visitor. I called all my neighbours, but none of them had seen him either. Next I phoned the SPCA. They said they'd contact me if Fernando showed up.

I didn't sleep well that night. I was sad and worried, and Peter kept sneezing kitty litter into my face. In the early morning I called Mum to tell her that Fernando was missing.

"Oh, well, he's daft," she said. "He'll come staggering down the driveway one day, you'll see." And after our conversation, the drama didn't seem so big.

I spent the day getting back into the rhythms of the farm. In the late afternoon, the phone rang. It was the SPCA. "A woman named Sharon found your dog," the SPCA person told me. The mood of Glamorgan Farm changed!

I called Sharon right away, and she said, "Oh, he's a dear. I work at FedEx at the airport, and I found him sitting at the end of the runway yesterday morning. We all love him."

How could Fernando have walked all the way to the airport? I wondered. But I was very excited to hear the news.

"If his owner hadn't showed up, the girls and I were going to keep him and name him FedRex," Sharon continued. "And I hope you don't mind, but we gave him a bath."

I got into the van and headed over to the airport, stopping first to pick up some homemade brownies, lemon squares, cinnamon buns and date bars at the Deep Cove Store. On a card featuring the work of a local artist I wrote, "Thank you to my new friends at FedEx. We will visit often. With love, Fernando and Anny."

The FedEx office was housed in a metal building with the big orange and purple logo up above. Sharon came out, dressed in her dark-blue FedEx uniform, and Fernando, very dapper, walked beside her. When he saw me, we had a little reunion—a lot of licking and hot breath and paws. Then he sat down regally at my feet as I gave Sharon the goodies I had brought.

The other FedEx women came out to say goodbye. I gave Sharon my address and told her and the others to come and visit Fernando any time. Then I attached the pretty rainbow collar that the SPCA had given Fernando, and he followed me loyally out to the van. I had to help him in. The Old Gals and Alice Mary greeted their pal in the driveway. Even Peter looked pleased to see his fellow SPCA friend home.

The next day I had my chimneys cleaned and related the story to the sooty chimney sweep. He loved dogs and petted Fernando as he sniffed the tray of wire brushes and scraper devices. The sweep chuckled and, as he pulled his ladder from the back of his pickup truck quipped, "He's a special dog to go and meet you at the airport, and on the runway no less."

And that's when I realized that that was exactly what Fernando had done. I pictured him, determined, in his devoted little mind, to meet my plane, heading off through the tall grass and buttercups on his feeble, thin hips, across the airport fields; even more mysterious—he was on time, and Air Canada was two hours late!

TouchWood Editions
#108–17665 66A Avenue
Surrey, BC V3S 2A7
www.touchwoodeditions.com

PO Box 468
Custer, WA
98240-0468

LIBRARY AND ARCHIVES CANADA CATALOGUING IN PUBLICATION

Scoones, Anny, 1957–

   Home and away: more tales of a heritage farm / Anny Scoones.

ISBN-13: 978-1-894898-49-2
ISBN-10:1-894898-49-4

   1. Glamorgan Farm (North Saanich, B.C.)—Anecdotes. 2. Scoones, Anny, 1957–
—Anecdotes. 3. Farm life—British Columbia—North Saanich—Anecdotes. 4. Historic
farms—British Columbia—North Saanich—Anecdotes. I. Title.

S522.C3S36 2006   C818'.603   C2006-905342-1

LIBRARY OF CONGRESS CONTROL NUMBER: 2006907470

Edited by Barbara Pulling and Marlyn Horsdal
Proofread by Jonathan Dore
Book design and layout by Jacqui Thomas
Paintings by Molly Lamb Bobak, Bruno Bobak and Harold Mortimer-Lamb
Front-cover image by PhotoGen-X/iStockphoto; back-cover photos by Jacqui Thomas

Printed and bound in Canada by Friesens

TouchWood Editions acknowledges the financial support for its publishing program
from the Government of Canada through the Book Publishing Industry Development
Program (BPIDP), Canada Council for the Arts, and the province of British Columbia
through the British Columbia Arts Council and the Book Publishing Tax Credit.